Rather than fall into the trap of insisting on one 'theory' of the atonement, John Calvin recognised that the biblical teaching presents us with a multi-faceted jewel. His brilliant exposition stressed the many-sidedness and the profundity of the work of Christ. The great strength of Dr Robert Peterson's work lies in his grasp of Calvin's biblical vision and the clarity and enthusiasm with which he expounds it. Sixteen years after its first publication this revised edition of *Calvin and the Atonement* will be welcomed by a new generation of readers.

Sinclair B. Ferguson.
St George's Tron Church, Glasgow

Calvin and the Atonement

Robert A Peterson

MENTOR

ISBN 978 1 84550 377 3

This edition published in 1999, reprinted in 2009 in the
Mentor imprint
by
Christian Focus Publications, Geanies House,
Fearn, Ross-shire, IV20 1TW, Scotland.

www.christianfocus.com

Cover Design by Owen Daily

Printed and bound by Bell and Bain

Contents

I affectionately dedicate this book to my mother,
Marjorie Peterson.

FOREWORD

It has come to be expected that 'theories of the atonement' (to use the familiar nineteenth-century phrase) will put forward a single integrating concept towards which, so they claim, all the varied biblical descriptions of Christ's saving achievement point: some such concept as satisfaction for sin, or the reconciling of estranged friends, or the display of God's fatherly love, or victory over all evil. It is true that many accounts of Jesus' saviourhood have been constructed in this way, but in their attempts to go behind, beyond and above Scripture in their integrating purpose, they have regularly fallen short of Scripture in its breadth and many-sidedness of teaching.

When in 1977 a learned man began an article with the words, 'Calvin's theory of the atonement is basically ....,' he was forcing Calvin into a mold of this kind, and thereby pulling his thought out of shape. For in fact Calvin dealt with Christ's saving ministry, as with all other biblical themes, in a different way. He wove into a single texture all the strands of thought and imagery on the subject that he found in Scripture, treating it all as God's own teaching given through his human spokesmen, and in both the *Institutes* and the commentaries he achieved an extraordinarily rich synthesis of this material.

Dr. Peterson's monograph lays out the elements of this synthesis in a way that Calvin himself would certainly have approved. The task has not been tackled in print before in so adequate a manner, and this essay is something of a milestone. I commend it heartily, both as a fine contribution to modern Calvin studies and as a worthy presentation of insights into a central theme of Scripture from one of the greatest Bible expositors of all time.

J.I. Packer
Regent College

PREFACE

The twentieth century has witnessed a renaissance in Calvin research. Important contributions have been made in the areas of Calvin's understanding of the knowledge of God, predestination, the church, and the sacraments. Some other areas have not fared as well. Calvin's doctrine of the work of Christ has not received the attention it deserves. In 1957 Paul Van Buren penned a valuable work entitled *Christ in Our Place: The Substitutionary Character of Calvin's Doctrine of Reconciliation.*[1] Van Buren included the incarnation, the atonement, and union with Christ in his book. He very capably set the parameters for further work on Calvin's doctrine of Christ's work. And yet, because his scope was large, his treatment of the saving work of Christ left more to be done. Van Buren presented only three of Calvin's six biblical themes of the atonement (obedience, law, and sacrifice). He also omitted the relation of the threefold office of Christ to the biblical themes of Christ's work.

Both J.F. Jansen and K. Blaser wrote books presenting Christ's threefold office of prophet, king, and priest.[2] Neither, however, included the biblical pictures of the atonement in his work. Consequently, although they put forth valuable material, they offered only a partial picture of Calvin's understanding of Christ's saving work.

Charles Hall did a good job of describing Calvin's victory theme of the atonement in his publication of 1970.[3] Once again,

---

1. Paul Van Buren, *Christ in Our Place: The Substitutionary Character of Calvin's Doctrine of Reconciliation* (Grand Rapids: Eerdmans, 1975).
2. John F. Jansen, *Calvin's Doctrine of the Work of Christ* (London: J. Clarke, 1956), and Klauspeter Blaser, *Calvins Lehre von den drei Ämtern Christi*, Theologische Studien, vol. 105 (Zürich: EVZ-Verlag, 1970).
3. Charles A. M. Hall, *With the Spirit's Sword: The Drama of Spiritual Warfare in the Theology of John Calvin*, Basel Studies of Theology, no. 3 (Richmond: John Knox, 1970).

however, this book only captured a portion of the whole of Calvin's thought concerning the atonement.

I have written to fill a gap in the Calvin literature. This is the first book to present the doctrine of the atonement the way Calvin did: in terms of both the threefold office of Christ and the six biblical themes of the work of Christ. As a result, Calvin's teaching can be appreciated as one of the most comprehensive presentations of the work of Christ in the history of Christian doctrine.

In the course of this book it will be evident that I agree with H. Jackson Forstman's estimate of John Calvin as 'a biblical theologian par excellence'.[4] Because he sought diligently to base his theology upon the exegesis of Scripture, Calvin's treatment of the work of Christ has importance for students of biblical and systematic theology, as well as for historical theologians.

I wish to express my appreciation to those gracious people who have assisted me in the production of this work. I thank Kenilworth Gospel Chapel of Kenilworth, New Jersey, for allowing their assistant pastor to devote his mornings to the completion of this book. To Drs. Bard Thompson, James Pain, and Kenneth Rowe of Drew University, who comprised a most helpful and cooperative dissertation committee, I acknowledge a debt of gratitude. I thank Professor Thomas Taylor and former Assistant Librarian John Pickard of Biblical Theological Seminary of Hatfield, Pennsylvania, for their labors of love in reading the manuscript. Special thanks is due James Pakala, the librarian of Biblical Theological Seminary, for his painstaking efforts in correcting the bibliography and footnotes.

I wish to express appreciation to my students who have helped in the reading of the manuscript: James Bordwine, David Hudson, Bradley Mellon, Joseph Murphy, and Albert Tricarico.

I thank my wife, Mary Pat, for her constant encouragement; without her love this work would not have been written.

Most of all I thank the Lord Jesus Christ, 'who loved me and delivered himself up for me' (Gal. 2:20), and who 'considered me faithful, putting me into service' (1 Tim. 1:12)

4. H. Jackson Forstman, *Word and Spirit: Calvin's Doctrine of Biblical Authority* (Stanford, Calif.: Stanford Univ. Press, 1962), p. 30.

PREFACE TO NEW EDITION

I am thankful to God for the opportunity to write a revised edition of *Calvin's Doctrine of the Atonement*. It is difficult for me to believe that sixteen years have passed since the first edition appeared. This edition represents my attempt to take into account the books and articles written between 1983 and 1999. I have learned from them and have incorporated new insights in the text, notes, and above all in the conclusion, which has been rewritten.

I owe a debt of gratitude to persons who have helped me accomplish this task. I thank my colleagues David B. Calhoun and Michael D. Williams for taking time from busy schedules to read parts of the manuscript and to make suggestions. I thank my student assistant, Jonathan Barlow, for three faithful years of service, exemplified in his help on this work. I thank Malcolm Maclean, Managing Editor of Christian Focus Publications, for his support, patience, and encouragement. I thank my wife Mary Pat, and our sons Robby, Matt, Curtis, and David for their love and prayers.

I am happy to dedicate this book to my wonderful mother, Marjorie Peterson, as I did in 1983. Most of all, now as then, I thank Jesus Christ for loving me and giving himself for me (Gal. 2:20) and for considering me faithful, appointing me to his service (1 Tim. 1:12). To him be the glory.

Covenant Theological Seminary, St. Louis
February 1999

1

THE STARTING POINT:

THE FREE LOVE OF GOD IN JESUS CHRIST

'He is moved by pure and freely given love of us to receive us into grace.... Therefore, by his love God the Father goes before and anticipates our reconciliation in Christ' (*Inst.* II.xvi.3).

Opinions vary as to what theological truth is most foundational to Calvin's doctrine of the atonement. One suggestion is Calvin's Christology: one cannot understand the work of the Mediator without first understanding the person of Christ. The structure of Calvin's *Institutes of the Christian Religion* offers support for that suggestion. The chapters in the *Institutes* that tell of Christ's person (II. xii-xiv) directly precede chapters II. xv-xvii, which tell of his saving work. It must be admitted that Christology is foundational to soteriology. Yet Christology is not the theological starting point for the atonement in Calvin.

One could move further back theologically and speak of Calvin's doctrine of sin as the place to begin. Since, for Calvin, original sin leaves no room for the efforts of sinners to rescue themselves from God's judgment,[1] Christ's atoning work is necessary for salvation. Again, the organization of the *Institutes* lends credence to such a suggestion.[2] But while Calvin's doctrine

---

1. 'Original sin, therefore, seems to be a hereditary depravity and corruption of our nature, diffused into all parts of the soul, which first makes us liable to God's wrath, then also brings forth in us those works which Scripture calls "works of the flesh" (Gal. 5:19)' (John Calvin, *Institutes of the Christian Religion*, ed. John T. McNeill, 2 vols., The Library of Christian Classics, vols. 20-21 [Philadelphia: Westminster, 1960], II. i. 8).
2. Calvin's doctrine of sin is found in *Institutes* II. i-v. Then in II. vi Calvin announces, 'Fallen Man Ought to Seek Redemption in Christ.'

of sin is theologically prior to his doctrine of atonement, it is still not the best starting point for that doctrine.

One must reach back to the eternal counsels of the triune God to locate the ultimate source of Calvin's doctrine of Christ's work. The *free love of God in Jesus Christ* is the starting point for Calvin's doctrine of the atonement. In his commentary on John 3:16, Calvin specifies as much: 'Christ shows the first cause and as it were source of our salvation. And this He does that no doubt may be left. For there is no calm haven where our minds can rest until we come to God's free love.'[3] In numerous other places in his commentaries Calvin insists that the free love of God in Christ is the starting point for redemption:

> The ground of our redemption is that immense love of God towards us by which it happened that He did not even spare His own Son.
>
> For it is not true (as some carelessly make out) that repentance is put in first place, as though it were the cause of the remission of sins, or came before God's starting to be well-favoured towards us, but men are told to repent that they may perceive the reconciliation that is offered to them. As first in rank comes the free love of God, in which He embraces poor men, not imputing their sins to them.[4]

Moreover, the love of God plays an important role in the theology of John Calvin as a whole. His comments on John's words, 'By this the love of God was manifested,' are especially apt:

---

3. Cf. Paul Van Buren, *Christ in Our Place: The Substitutionary Character of Calvin's Doctrine of Reconciliation* (Grand Rapids: Eerdmans, 1957), pp. 8f.
4. Calvin's commentaries on Heb. 2:9 and Matt. 3:2. When this theological starting point for Calvin's soteriology is overlooked, he is misunderstood. He is said to have added 'some abhorrent features' in systematizing the Reformation doctrine (see G. C. Foley, *Anselm's Theory of the Atonement* [New York: Longman's, Green, and Co., 1909], p. 225). Calvin is even accused of leaving no place for Christ in his predestinarian scheme (so Adam M. Hunter, *The Teaching of Calvin: A Modern Interpretation*, 2nd ed. [London: J. Clarke, 1950], p. 111).

> The love of God is testified to us by many other proofs as well. For if it is asked why the world was created, why we have been put in it to have dominion over the earth, why we are preserved in this life to enjoy innumerable blessings and are endowed with light and understanding, no reason can be given but the free love of God towards us. But here the apostle chooses the chief example, which transcends everything else .... Christ is such a shining and remarkable proof of the divine love towards us, that, whenever we look to Him, He clearly confirms to us the doctrine that God is love.[5]

When Calvin formulates a minimal confession of faith necessary for church union, he includes the love of God: 'God is one; Christ is God and the Son of God; our salvation rests in God's mercy.'[6] Erwin Mülhaupt, who did painstaking work in studying Calvin's sermons, underscored the importance of love for Calvin's practical theology: 'A study of Calvin's sermons reveals that it is not his ideas of law, but the lovingkindness of God which predominates.'[7]

The best witness to the importance of love in Calvin's theology is his own in his exegesis of Ephesians 3:17f. ('That you, being rooted and grounded in love, may be able to comprehend with all the saints what is the breadth and length and height and depth, and to know the love of Christ ....'):

> By these dimensions Paul means nothing other than the love of Christ, of which he speaks afterwards. The meaning is, that he who knows it truly and perfectly is in every respect a wise man. As if he had said, 'In whatever direction men may look, they will find nothing in the doctrine of salvation that should not be related to this.' The love of Christ contains within itself every aspect of wisdom.[8]

---

5. Calvin's commentary on 1 John 4:9.
6. *Institutes* IV. i. 12. Cf. Joachim Staedtke, *Johannes Calvin: Erkenntnis und Gestaltung*, Persönlichkeit and Geschichte (Göttingen: Musterschmidt-Verlag, 1969), p. 85.
7. Erwin Mülhaupt, *Die Predigt Calvins, ihre Geschichte, ihre Form und ihre religiösen Grundgedanken* (Berlin: DeGruyter, 1931), p. 151.
8. Calvin's commentary on Eph. 3:18. For an extended discussion of God's love in Calvin, see Edward A. Dowey, *The Knowledge of God in Calvin's Theology* (New York: Columbia U. Pr., 1952), pp. 205-9.

When Calvin says that God's love is *free*, he means that there is no necessity for God to direct his love toward sinners. God is sovereign; he acts because he chooses to act. And there is nothing in sinful men and women to constrain God to love them. God loves freely, as Calvin relates in his commentary on Titus 3:4: '[Paul] is right to mention first the kindness that prompts God to love us. He will never find in us anything worthy of His love, but He loves us because He is kind and merciful.'[9]

When Calvin tells of 'free love', he emphasizes not only God's freedom but his great *love* for his people. That love is demonstrated in creation, in providence, and above all, in redemption. Therefore, Calvin's phrase 'the free love of God' includes an adjective describing the *sovereignty* of God's love and a noun depicting His *lovingkindness*.

It is important to note that Christ is inseparable from this love of God; God's free love is *in Jesus Christ* and comes to believers through Christ. Calvin, in his commentaries, speaks of Christ as a 'fountain' of God's grace:

> But it accords beautifully with Christ clothed in flesh that He is loved by the Father. Nay, we know that it is by this pre-eminent title that He is distinguished from both angels and men: 'This is my beloved Son' (Matt. 3:17). And we know that Christ was chosen that the whole love of God might dwell in Him, so as to flow from Him to us as from a full fountain.
>
> He is the beloved Son in whom the Father is well pleased (Matt. 3:17). If, therefore, we cleave to God by Him, we are assured of God's inflexible and unwearied kindness towards us. Paul now speaks here more plainly than above, placing the fountain of love in the Father, and affirming that it flows to us from Christ.[10]

By means of the biblical concept of adoption, Calvin connects the love of God and the person of Christ. In the *Institutes* he discusses at length how the God-man is the source of adoption. Again and again Calvin expresses the basic idea: God became a

---

9. Cf. the statement in Calvin's commentary on Rom. 5:8.
10. Calvin's commentaries on John 5:20 and Rom. 8:39.

man and thereby took what was ours (humanity) to impart to us what was his (salvation). He, the Son of God, became a Son of man that we, children of men and heirs of Gehenna, might become sons and daughters of God. Therein is our adoption.[11]

Calvin presents his doctrine of adoption in his commentary on Matthew 3:17, where the Father speaks from heaven at Christ's baptism, saying, 'This is My beloved Son, in whom I am well pleased':

> Further, Christ was presented to us by the Father with this proclamation, in His coming forth to fulfill His task of Mediator, that we might rely on this pledge of our adoption and without fear call God Himself our Father. The title of Son truly and by nature belongs to Christ alone, yet He was revealed as Son of God in our flesh, that He who alone claimed Him as Father by right, could win Him for us also. So God, in introducing our Mediator with words that praise Him as the Son, declares Himself to be a Father to us all. This is exactly the aim of the word *beloved*, for as in ourselves we are hateful to God, His fatherly love must flow to us in Christ.[12]

This quotation contains another of Calvin's favorite expressions to describe how Christ is intimately bound up with God's love for his people. Jesus is 'the pledge of our adoption', 'a pledge of God's boundless love towards us',[13] and 'the pledge of God's fatherly mercy in redeeming us'.[14]

Jesus Christ is so closely joined to the free love of God for sinners that he too is said to love them. Indeed, at times Calvin expressed the love of God as the love of Christ.[15] In Christ's

---

11. *Institutes* II. xii. 2.
12. Cf. his comments on 2 Cor. 1:10 and John 20:17.
13. Calvin's commentary on Rom. 8:32.
14. Calvin's commentary on John 10:17. See his comments on 2 Cor. 1:10 and John 3:16 for outstanding statements of God's love for his people in Christ. Cf. Heribert Schützeichel, *Die Glaubenstheologie Calvins*, Beiträge zur ökumenischen Theologie (München: Hueber, 1972), 9:165.
15. 'So also God's inestimable mercy upon us shines out, in lowering His only-begotten Son to these depths, for our sake. By this proof

humiliation and condescension Calvin finds the greatest demonstration of his love for his people. This humiliation began when Christ entered the world by becoming a man.[16] Love was the characteristic attribute of the Savior's earthly life.[17] Christ's condescension, the proof of his love for sinners, was supremely displayed in his giving himself in death for his people. Calvin's commentaries abundantly testify to this fact.[18]

We have described the love of God in Calvin's thought as the *free* love of God. We need to explore further Calvin's doctrine of predestination as it relates to God's love. For Calvin, God's election of a people for himself is purely an act of grace. It is striking to see how Calvin frequently combines God's love and election.[19]

Christ witnessed to His amazing love for us, in refusing no insult at all for our salvation' (Calvin's commentary on Matt. 27:27). Cf. Robert S. Paul, *The Atonement and the Sacraments: The Relation of the Atonement to the Sacraments of Baptism and the Lord's Supper* (New York: Abingdon, 1960), pp. 108f.

16. Calvin's comments on John 6:41 are especially apt: 'But we are very ill-disposed if we despise the Lord of glory because He emptied Himself and took the form of a servant for our sake. Rather was this the shining example of His boundless love toward us and of His wonderful grace.' Cf. Max Dominicé, *L'humanité de Jesus d'après Calvin* (Paris: Je Sers, 1933), p. 71.

17. See Calvin's comments on Mark 7:32 for a demonstration of Christ's 'singular love towards men.' Cf. Dominicé, p. 52.

18. 'The Lord has given no ordinary proof of His love towards the Church, by pouring out His own blood for its sake' (Calvin's commentary on Acts 20:28). 'Let us observe the order, "He loved us and gave Himself for us." It is as if He said, 'He had no other reason for dying than because He loved us,' and that when we were enemies, as He says in Rom. 5:10' (Calvin's commentary on Gal. 2:20). 'It was a remarkable proof of the highest love that forgetful, as it were, of Himself, Christ spared not His own life, that He might redeem us from death' (Calvin's commentary on Eph. 5:2).

19. Dowey wrote, 'For Calvin, God is never merely sovereign, He is sovereignly good, sovereignly just, sovereignly merciful and gracious' (Dowey, pp. 210f.).

A careful reading of the first chapter that deals with election in the *Institutes* (III. xxi) reveals how frequently Calvin mentions the love of God in reference to predestination. Calvin assures his readers, 'We shall never be clearly persuaded, as we ought to be, that our salvation flows from the wellspring of God's free mercy until we come to know his eternal election.' Further on he writes, 'To make it clear that our salvation comes about solely from God's mere generosity – we must be called back to the course of election.'[20] Believers of the Old Testament, as well as those of the New, should have known 'that they excel solely by God's freely given love.' God's people must ever be reminded that their election rests upon 'the remarkable generosity of his fatherly benevolence',[21] 'God's special grace', 'the marvelous secrets of God's grace', 'his mere generosity',[22] 'God's generous favor', and 'his freely given mercy'.[23] It is significant that Calvin's first chapter on election, which sets the tone for his whole discussion of that doctrine, is replete with references to the love of God. The conclusion is the same when one reads the key *loci* from Calvin's commentaries: God's eternal predestination of his people for salvation is inseparable from his love.[24]

---

20. *Institutes* III. xxi. 1.
21. Ibid., III. xxi. 5.
22. Ibid., III xxi. 6.
23. Ibid., III. xxi. 7.
24. 'The Father by His eternal purpose decreed this atonement and in it gave this proof of His love for us that He spared not His only-begotten Son, but delivered Him up for us all' (Calvin's commentary on Gal. 1:4). 'By this he tells us that God embraces us in His love and favour freely and not on a wages basis, just as, when we were not yet born, and when He was prompted by nothing but Himself, He chose us' (Calvin's commentary on Eph. 1:5). When Calvin's doctrine of election is separated from his emphasis on God's love, great misunderstanding results. He has been accused of presenting God as an 'autocratic deity of the old dispensation.' His doctrine of election 'could never be wholly brought into line with the teaching of the Gospel.' In fact, Calvin has little need in his system for the 'gracious and loving God of the New Testament' (Robert N. C. Hunt, *Calvin* [London: Centenary, 1933],

The relationship between God's love and his wrath makes a worthwhile study in Calvin's theology. Time and again in both the *Institutes* and the commentaries, Calvin refers to 'some sort of contradiction', or 'inconsistency' between the love and wrath of God.[25] The problem is summarized well by Calvin in his commentary on Romans 5:10.

> We were enemies, he says, when Christ presented Himself to the Father as a means of propitiation .... The apostle, however, seems here to be contradicting himself. If the death of Christ was a pledge of the divine love towards us, it follows that we were even then acceptable to Him. But now he says that we were enemies.[26]

---

p. 122). Some have faulted Calvin for not properly relating Christ to election. Schellong tells us that the decree of God is not anchored in Christ (see Dieter Schellong, *Calvins Auslegung der synoptischen Evangelien*, ed. Ernst Wolf, Forschungen zur Geschichte und Lehre des Protestantismus, ser. 10 [München: C. Kaiser, 1969], p. 247f.). Although it is true that most often Calvin anchors election in the will of God the Father, at least three times – once in the *Institutes* (III. xxii. 7) and twice in the commentaries (John 13:18; 15:16) – he teaches that, 'Christ is the author of election.'

25. *Institutes* II. xvi. 2, and Calvin's commentary on 1 John 4:10. Cf. Calvin's commentaries on John 17:23, Rom. 5:10, and 2 Cor. 5:19.

26. Various attempts have been made to resolve this problem in Calvin's thought. Some attack his attempt to 'keep in harmony two entirely contradictory ideas' and conclude that, as a result, Calvin makes placation 'utterly meaningless' (Foley, p. 222). Cf. Charles A. M. Hall, *With the Spirit's Sword: The Drama of Spiritual Warfare in the Theology of John Calvin*, Basel Studies of Theology, no. 3 (Richmond: John Knox, 1970), p. 103. Others do not view it as a serious problem at all. Calvin can 'without difficulty' maintain this paradox because its resolution is in Christ's work on the cross (see Marvin P. Hoogland, 'Calvin's Perspective on the Exaltation of Christ in Comparison with the Post-Reformation Doctrine of the Two States' [Th.D. diss., Free University of Amsterdam, 1966], p. 137. Cf. Van Buren, pp. 58f.). Some scholars stress the places where Calvin seems to resolve this tension by distinguishing divine and human points of view. Hence this is an example of accommodation in

It is important to consider Calvin's appeals to divine and human viewpoints in this matter. In a key passage in the *Institutes*, after posing the contradiction and concluding with passages of Scripture that stress God's wrath, Calvin writes:

> Expressions of this sort have been accommodated to our capacity that we may better understand how miserable and ruinous our condition is apart from Christ. For if it had not been clearly stated that the wrath and vengeance of God and eternal death rested upon us, we would scarcely have recognised how miserable we would have been without God's mercy, and we would have underestimated the benefit of liberation .... To sum up: since our hearts cannot, in God's mercy, either seize upon life ardently enough or accept it with the gratefulness we owe, unless our minds are first struck and overwhelmed by fear of God's wrath and by dread of eternal death, we are taught by Scripture to perceive that apart from Christ, God

---

Calvin and the problem is only an apparent one (see François Wendel, *Calvin: Origins and Development of His Religious Thought*, trans. Philip Mairet [New York: Har-Row, 1963], p. 230, and George H. Kehm, 'Calvin on Defilement and Sacrifice,' *Interpretation* 31 [1977]: 49). Still others have laid stress on the concept of mystery. Calvin allowed the biblical tension to remain. The cross is no answer, but it highlights the mystery (see Tjarko Stadtland, *Rechtfertigung und Heiligung bei Calvin*, Beiträge zur Geschichte und Lehre der Reformierten Kirche [Neukirchen-Vluyn: Neukirchener Verlag, 1972], p. 141, and G. C. Berkouwer, *The Work of Christ*, Studies in Dogmatics [Grand Rapids: Eerdmans, 1965], pp. 268-70).

Those who attack the very notion of a love/wrath dialectic seem insensitive to the biblical witness, and consequently adopt a posture from which they cannot appreciate Calvin's thought at this point. The cross of Christ is central to the problem. It is here God's love is displayed and his wrath appeased. But it is too simple to appeal to the cross as that which solves the problem. Accommodation has an important place in Calvin's thought, but it is not the final answer to this dilemma. It cannot be, for Calvin takes seriously God's wrath and human sin. The element of mystery must be appreciated, but it too is not the complete solution. It must be viewed in the context of God's electing love being set upon those who deserve only his wrath.

> is, so to speak, hostile to us, and his hand is armed for our destruction, to embrace his benevolence and fatherly love in Christ alone.[27]

There is no doubt that accommodation is an important concept in Calvin's theology.[28] Calvin emphasizes it in the discussions of the love/wrath dilemma not only in the *Institutes*, but also in the commentaries.[29] And yet accommodation can be overemphasized to the place where God's wrath loses its reality. Calvin is careful not to do this. Accommodation is only a partial answer for the Reformer – it did not negate God's wrath.

> For God who is the highest righteousness, cannot love the unrighteousness that he sees in us all. All of us, therefore, have in ourselves something deserving of God's hatred. With regard to our corrupt nature and the wicked life that follows it, all of us surely displease God, are guilty in his sight, and are born to the damnation of hell.[30]

It is of utmost importance to note that this passage, which affirms the reality of God's wrath, immediately follows the passage quoted above in which Calvin speaks of accommodation as a partial solution to the problem. Accommodation is not the final answer. It cannot be, because Calvin takes the holiness of God and the sinfulness of men and women with utter seriousness.

In working through the love/wrath problem in Calvin, the first thing that must be said is this: God is righteous and hates sinners. The second thing is that in his eternal counsels God freely willed to save the elect; he set his love upon those who deserved only his wrath. Two things must be stressed in conjunction with this second point. One is the element of mystery. This love 'was hidden

---

27. *Institutes* II. xvi. 2.
28. See an introduction to this concept in Calvin's thought by Ford Lewis Battles, 'God Was Accommodating Himself to Human Capacity,' *Interpretation* 31 (1977): 19-38.
29. Cf. Calvin's commentaries on 2 Cor. 5:19 and 1 John 4:10.
30. *Institutes* II. xvi. 3.

in the bosom of God and far exceeds the grasp of the human mind.' Indeed, 'it is a wonderful goodness of God and incomprehensible to the human mind, that He was benevolent towards men whom He could not but hate.'[31] This love is 'by His secret counsel.'[32] It is 'the secret love which ... flows from His eternal good pleasure.'[33] Calvin quotes Augustine, 'In some ineffable way, God loved us and yet was angry toward us at the same time.'[34]

The second thing to be emphasized, and the more important in terms of the thought of this chapter, is that God's love precedes our salvation in Christ: 'By his love God the Father goes before and anticipates our reconciliation in Christ.'[35] Here at the conclusion of this chapter we return to the place we began. The love of God is the best starting point for understanding Calvin's doctrine of the atonement. 'Because he first loved us (1 John 4:19), he afterward reconciles us to himself.'[36] The 'secret love in which our heavenly Father embraced us to Himself is ... precedent to all other causes.'[37]

If it were not for the precedent love of God, there would be no salvation. God took the initiative and loved those whom he hated because of their sins. Here is the place for accommodation in this discussion. Having spoken of the reality of God's wrath against sinners and the eternal mystery of his love for the elect, which precedes their salvation, one can speak of Christians' apprehension of God's love in Christ. 'Our return to grace ... is unknown to us, until we attain it by faith.'[38] God revealed his love for us when he was reconciled to us by Christ's blood.[39] 'None will ever feel that God is favorable to him unless he understands that

31. Calvin's commentary on John 17:23.
32. Calvin's commentary on Rom. 5:10.
33. Calvin's commentary on John 3:16.
34. *Institutes* II. xvii. 2. Cf. ibid., II. xvi. 4.
35. Ibid., II. xvi. 3.
36. Ibid.
37. Calvin's commentary on John 3:16.
38. Calvin's commentary on Rom. 5:10.
39. *Institutes* II. xvii. 2.

God is appeased in Christ.'[40] Sinners learn of God's anger against them and this drives them to Christ as their only escape. In Christ they see God's love for them and experience the forgiveness of sins by faith. God loved his people before the worlds were made, but they experience his love in their life stories only through faith in Christ.

God loved sinful men and women before he was reconciled to them and they to him by his Son's death in their place. His love was the reason he sent his Son to die for them. But God also was angry at them until his Son removed the cause of that anger. Calvin, therefore, proclaims:

> We are loved in a double sense: first, because the Father chose us in Him before the creation of the world (Eph. 1:4). Secondly, because in Him also God has reconciled us to Himself and shown that He is gracious to us (Rom. 5:10). See how we are both enemies and friends until atonement has been made for our sins and we are restored to favour with God![41]

40. Calvin's commentary on John 17:23.
41. Ibid.

2

THE PREREQUISITE FOR ATONEMENT:

THE INCARNATION

'Christ had to become man in order to fulfill
the office of Mediator' (*Inst.* II. xii).

In the thought of John Calvin there is an essential precondition for the atonement; without it no atonement could have been accomplished. It is likewise that which makes the atonement intelligible – it gives Christ's work its meaning and force. That prerequisite for atonement in Calvin is the incarnation: *God became a human being for our salvation.* When we understand the meaning and ramifications of that statement, we will be ready to examine the atonement itself.

God Became a Human Being for Our Salvation

John Calvin affirms the full deity of the Mediator, Jesus Christ. Christ is of the very essence of God.[1] Calvin holds that Christ is 'truly and essentially God'.[2] Indeed, 'the whole God is found in Him so that he who is not satisfied with Christ alone, desires something better and more excellent than God.'[3]

Calvin's strong affirmation of the essential deity of Christ is better appreciated alongside of Servetus' denial of the same.[4] It

---

1. 'But I extend it much further, in that Christ's power and grace, inasmuch as He is the Redeemer of the world, were common to all ages .... Yet that the grace of the Mediator flourished in all ages depended on His eternal divinity. And this saying of Christ contains a remarkable statement of His divine essence' (Calvin's commentary on John 8:58).
2. Calvin's commentary on Gen. 18:13. Cf. Calvin's commentary on Phil. 2:5.
3. Calvin's commentary on Col. 2:9.
4. Quotations will be limited to Servetus' works *On the Errors of the*

is no accident that the first mention of Servetus in the *Institutes* occurs in I. xiii. 10. Calvin has been discussing the doctrine of the Trinity, which leads him to devote I. xiii. 7-13 to the eternal deity of the Son of God. Here the name of Servetus first appears. Servetus opposes Calvin's teaching at every point, arguing that Christ 'is not God in Nature but in appearance ... for only the Father is called God by Nature.'[5] Servetus admits that Christ is God, but only in this manner: 'He is God, a kind of deity being shared by him with the Father.'[6] In other words, 'God can share with a man the fullness of his deity.'[7]

Calvin on the contrary teaches that Christ is fully God. He warned against denying the true deity (or humanity) of Christ; salvation is forfeited if Christ is not God:

> Since God so often promised that Christ would spring from the seed, from the loins of David, the idea was so firmly rooted in all Jewish minds that they could scarcely have allowed His human nature to be dispensed with. Satan allowed Christ to be acknowledged true

---

Trinity and *Dialogues on the Trinity*. Servetus' final work, *The Restitution of Christianity*, will not be used because of the facts brought to light by E. M. Wilbur: 'A word should be said in closing upon Servetus' last work, *Christianismi Restitutio*, published in 1553, which brought him to the stake .... Most writers upon the theology of Servetus have based their work upon this book. But while it is of high interest to any one wishing to trace the development of the author's thought, the whole edition was at once so nearly utterly destroyed that its historical influence may be considered negligible. In so far as Servetus had influence upon the course of religious thought in the reformation period or later, it was almost wholly due to the *Errors* and the *Dialogues*' (Michael Servetus, *The Two Treatises of Servetus on the Trinity*, trans. E. M. Wilbur, Harvard Theological Studies, no. 16 [Cambridge, Mass.: Harvard U. Pr., 1932], p. xviii).

5. Servetus, *The Two Treatises*, p. 21.

6. Ibid., p. 26.

7. Ibid., p. 19. See George H. Williams, *The Radical Reformation* (Philadelphia: Westminster, 1962), pp. 610ff., for a good summary of Servetus' Christology.

> man and Son of David, for it would have been useless to try to upset this leading article of faith, but (more grievously) he stripped Him of His Godhead, as if He should be any one at all of the sons of Adam. In this way the hope of eternal life to come and spiritual righteousness was done away.[8]

In the incarnation Jesus Christ is fully divine; none of his deity was set aside when the Word became flesh. Calvin affirms that God the Son was wholly incarnate in Jesus of Nazareth and yet wholly outside (*extra*) of him too. This is the *extra-calvinisticum*, the Calvinistic 'extra' or 'without'. God was 'without' Jesus as well as fully incarnate in him.[9]

There are two great passages in the *Institutes* where Calvin teaches the *extra-calvinisticum*. The first passage (IV. xvii. 30) is present in the first (1536) edition of the *Institutes* and grows to its expanded final form in the last (1559) edition. It is set in a context of eucharistic controversy.

> In this way he was also Son of man in heaven (John 3:13), for the very same Christ, who, according to the flesh, dwelt as Son of man on earth, was God in heaven. In this manner, he is said to have descended to that place according to his divinity, not because divinity left heaven to hide itself in the prison house of the body, but because

8. Calvin's commentary on Matt. 22:42. Cf. *Institutes* I. xiii. 13. For statements of Calvin's insistence on Christ's full deity, see Karl Barth, *La Confession de foi de l'église: Explication du Symbole des Apôtres d'après le catechisme de Calvin* (Neuchâtel: Delachaux et Niéstlé, 1943), p. 36; Wolfgang Kratz, 'Christus – Gott und Mensch: Einige Fragen an Calvins Christologie,' *Evangelische Theologie* 19 (1959): 210; and Wilhelm Hauck, *Christusglaube und Gottesoffenbarung nach Calvin* (Gütersloh: Bertelsmann, 1939), p. 73.

9. See the book by E. David Willis, *Calvin's Catholic Christology: The Function of the So-called 'Extra-Calvinisticum' in Calvin's Theology*, Studies in Medieval and Reformation Thought, vol. 2 (Leiden: Brill, 1966). For a presentation of other 'extras' in Calvin's thought, see Heiko A. Oberman, 'The "Extra" Dimension in the Theology of Calvin,' *The Journal of Ecclesiastical History* 21 (1970): 43-64.

> even though it filled all things, still in Christ's very humanity it dwelt bodily (Col. 2:9), that is, by nature and in a certain ineffable way.[10]

The other key text is found only in the 1559 edition of the *Institutes*, and it occurs in a context of Christological conflict. Calvin answers the charge of Menno Simons that if the Word of God became a man, 'then he was confined within the narrow prison of an earthly body'.[11]

> This is mere impudence! For even if the Word in his immeasurable essence united with the nature of man into one person, we do not imagine that he was confined therein. Here is something marvelous: the Son of God descended from heaven in such a way that, without leaving heaven, he willed to be borne in the virgin's womb, to go about the earth, and to hang upon the cross; yet he continuously filled the world even as he had done from the beginning![12]

---

10. *Institutes* IV. xvii. 30.
11. Menno Simons, *Complete Writings*, trans. Leonard Verduin, ed. John C. Wenger (Scottdale, Pa.: Herald Pr., 1956), pp. 881, 909. Hereafter cited as Verduin.
12. *Institutes* II. xiii. 4. Cf. Calvin's commentaries on Luke 23:43, John 14:12, Acts 1:11, and Heb. 1:14. The term *extra-calvinisticum* is a product of sixteenth- and seventeenth-century christological debates occasioned by the divergent views of Reformed and Lutheran theologians regarding the nature of Christ's presence in the Eucharist (Willis, pp. 8, 24f.). Yet the concept that 'the Eternal Son of God was united to but not restricted to his humanity' has 'a widespread and ancient usage'. Willis suggests the terms 'extra Catholicum' or 'extra Patristicum' as being more accurate than *extra-calvinisticum* (Willis, p. 60). This concept in Calvin's thought too often has been misunderstood. Some have felt that it impugns the reality of the incarnation (see H. R. Mackintosh, *The Doctrine of the Person of Jesus Christ*, International Theological Library [New York: Scribner, 1930], p. 244). Others have thought that it pushes Calvin in the direction of Nestorius (cf. J. S. Witte, 'Die Christologie Calvins', in *Das Konzil von Chalkedon: Geschichte und Gegenwart*, vol. 3: *Chalkedon Heute*, ed. Alois Grillmeier and Heinrich Bacht [Würzburg: Echter-Verlag, 1951-54], p. 506, and Uwe Gerber, 'Die Christologie bei Calvin', in *Christologische*

By espousing the *extra-calvinisticum* Calvin affirms both the deity of Christ and the incarnation of God the Son. It is the eternal God whom we meet in Jesus of Nazareth. As E. David Willis emphatically states:

> The *extra-calvinisticum* emphasizes that the God at work in Jesus Christ is one and the same with the God who sustains and orders the universe .... Calvin is asserting that Christ is able to be God for us because he does not cease to be God over us in the Incarnation and because the humanity of Christ never ceases to be our humanity in the movement of God towards us.[13]

The *extra-calvinisticum* does not open the door for a knowledge of God apart from the incarnate Word. Rather, it serves to safeguard the fact that 'in Jesus Christ we are faced not merely by enhanced nature, but the fact is that there God Himself stands revealed to us.'[14]

Calvin views the ascription of divine names and titles to Christ as further evidence of his deity. The angel who appeared to the patriarchs in the Old Testament 'claiming for himself the name of the Eternal God' was none other than the preincarnate Christ.[15] He is Immanuel ('God with us') in both Old Testament prediction and New Testament fulfillment.[16] He is called 'God' in Scripture.[17] When Servetus tries to deny the deity of Christ by claiming Scripture speaks of him only as Elohim but never as Jehovah,[18] Calvin counters with passages that clearly apply to Christ the

---

Entwürfe: Ein Arbeitsbuch, vol. 1, *Von der Reformation bis zur dialektischen Theologie* [Zürich: EVZ-Verlag, 1970], p. 3).

13. Willis, pp. 6f.

14. Wilhelm Niesel, *The Theology of Calvin*, trans. H. Knight (Philadelphia: Westminster, 1956), p. 119.

15. *Institutes* I. xiii. 10.

16. Calvin's commentaries on Isa. 7:14 and Matt. 1:23.

17. Calvin's commentaries on Ps. 45:6, Isa. 9:6. Cf. *Institutes* I. xiii. 9.

18. 'And that Christ became our God in the sense of the word, *Elohim*, is no more than to say that he became our Lord, our judge, and our king, after he was given by the Father a kingdom, all judgment, and all power ... and that Thomas spoke of Christ not as *Jehovah*, but as

tetragrammaton, which always indicated true deity to the Hebrews.[19] Finally, the name 'Son of God' speaks of the pre-incarnate divine essence of Christ and now applies to the two natures in one person.[20]

Calvin proclaims that 'God the Son did not deprive himself of any of his divine attributes even in becoming incarnate.'[21] He displayed the divine omnipotence that was his as 'the divine power shone out from the first in Christ.'[22] Jesus Christ exerted his omniscience by seeing within the hearts of his foes[23] and by forecasting future events.[24] Against Servetus,[25] Calvin affirms the eternity of the Son of God in both the *Institutes*[26] and the commentaries.[27]

Elohim and *Adonai*, I shall prove below' (Servetus, *The Two Treatises*, p. 23). Cf. ibid., p. 150.

19. 'This is Jehovah. It is worthy of observation that, when he calls Christ the God of believers, he gives to him the name 'Jehovah'; from which we infer that the actual eternity of God belongs to the person of Christ' (Calvin's commentary on Isa. 25:9). Cf. *Institutes* I. xii. 9.

20. Calvin's commentary on Luke 1:35. Cf. Calvin's commentary on Luke 1:32.

21. Ronald S. Wallace, *Calvin's Doctrine of the Word and Sacrament* (Grand Rapids: Eerdmans, 1957), pp. 14f.

22. Calvin's commentary on Luke 4:15. Cf. *Institutes* I. xiii. 12.

23. 'What? Does not the searching and penetrating of the silent thoughts of hearts belong to God alone? Yet Christ also had this power (Matt. 9:4). From this we infer his divinity' (*Institutes* I. xiii. 12). Cf. Calvin's commentary on Matt. 22:18.

24. Calvin's commentary on Matt. 21:2.

25. Servetus would allow Christ's eternity only in the sense that 'Christ was formed beforehand in the divine mind' (Servetus, *The Two Treatises*, p. 136). For Servetus, Christ was not eternal: 'There was then a Word concerning the being which now is; that is, the being itself did not exist, but there was a Word concerning it, like a conversation about an absent being, which was then represented by the Word' (Servetus, *The Two Treatises*, pp. 143f.). Cf. ibid., pp. 80, 84, 143, 172, 195.

26. 'Therefore nothing should be more intolerable to us than to fancy a beginning of that Word who both was always God and afterward was

Calvin holds that Christ demonstrated His deity by performing works belonging to God alone. In Scripture, only God is the Creator and Sustainer of the world, roles the writer to the Hebrews ascribes to Jesus Christ.[28] Servetus denied that Christ was the Creator.[29] In fact, his exegesis of Colossians 1:15 shows he held Christ to be 'a creature of God'.[30] How different is Calvin's exposition of the same passage, where he explained that Christ is called 'first-born' because he was 'the substance or foundation of all things'![31] Calvin views the miracles of Jesus Christ 'almost solely from the point of view of demonstration'.[32] He writes, 'How plainly and clearly is his deity shown in miracles!'[33] Calvin's commentaries on the Gospels abundantly testify to the sign-character of Christ's miracles. The miracles were 'testimonies to His divine power.'[34] Calvin explains: 'For we know that miracles were not some game that Christ was playing, but had the deliberate purpose of proving Him to be the Son of God and the Redeemer

---

the artificer of the universe .... Therefore we again state that the Word, conceived beyond the beginning of time by God, has perpetually resided with Him. By this, his eternity, his true essence, and his divinity are proven' (*Institutes* I. xiii. 8).

27. 'Though He was manifested Son of God in the flesh, it does not follow that He was not the Word begotten of the Father before all ages. No rather, He is the same, who was Son of God in the eternal Godhead, that appeared also Son of God in human flesh' (Calvin's commentary on Luke 1:35). Cf. Calvin's commentaries on Matt. 23:37, and 1 John 1:1, 2.

28. *Institutes* I. xii. 12. Cf. Calvin's commentaries on John 1:1, 5.

29. Servetus, *The Two Treatises*, p. 114.

30. 'Again, note this: that when Christ is called the first-born among creatures, he is also noted as being himself the creature of God' (Servetus, *The Two Treatises*, pp. 81f.).

31. Calvin's commentary on Col. 1:15.

32. Max Dominicé, *L'humanité de Jésus d'après Calvin*, p. 54. Cf. Wallace, p. 18, and Kratz, p. 212.

33. *Institutes* I. xiii. 13. Cf. ibid., I. xiii. 12.

34. Calvin's commentary on John 2:11. Cf. Calvin's commentaries on Luke 5:6, John 15:24, and 1 John 1:1.

given to the world.'[35] The greatest miracle of Christ is his resurrection. 'No greater proof of the divine powers in Christ could be desired.'[36] In his resurrection 'Christ was declared to be the Son of God by the open exercise of a truly heavenly power.' This 'proved beyond doubt that He was God.'[37] Commenting on John 2:19, Calvin says, 'Here Christ claims for Himself the glory of His resurrection, though generally in Scripture it is declared to be the work of the Father.'[38]

Since Jesus Christ is of the very essence of God, bears the titles and names of God, exercises the attributes of God, and does the works of God, 'that adoration which is proper to God' cannot be withheld from him.[39] Worship is due the Lord Jesus Christ because he is God. Above all, worship is due him because he performs the divine work of redemption. *God* became a human being *for our salvation*. After recording the account of Christ's healing the infirm man by the pool of Bethesda, Calvin points to the soteriological implications of Christ's deity:

> Christ now leaves His defense of this case and explains the purpose and use of the miracle as a means whereby He might be known as the Son of God. For in all His deeds and words His purpose was to show that He was the author of salvation .... And the reason why He declares He is God is that He, manifested in the flesh, might execute the office of the Christ.[40]

God Became *a Human Being* for Our Salvation

The true humanity of Christ is as important for our salvation as his true deity. The chapter title of *Institutes* II. xii bears this out: 'Christ Had to Become Man in Order to Fulfill the Office of

35. Calvin's commentary on Matt. 12:16.
36. Calvin's commentary on John 2:19.
37. Calvin's commentary on Rom. 1:4.
38. Calvin's commentary on John 2:19.
39. Calvin's commentary on Phil. 2:9.
40. Calvin's commentary on John 5:17. Cf. Calvin's commentary on John 20:31 and Willem F. Dankbaar, *Calvin: sein Weg und sein Werk* (Neukirchen: Neukirchener Verlag, 1959), p. 196.

Mediator.' The next chapter title is just as important: 'Christ Assumed the True Substance of Human Flesh.'

In chapter xiii Calvin wages war with those who deny the true humanity of Christ. His foes are both ancient (Marcion and the Manichees) and modern (Menno Simons). It is unclear how and when Calvin becomes aware of the Christology of Melchior Hofmann.[41] The Hofmannite view of Christ was passed on to Menno by Obbe Philips.[42] Menno teaches that since 'a woman has no procreative seed', Christ 'did not become flesh of Mary, but in Mary'.[43] Hence Christ's flesh 'is of the Holy Ghost ... not of Abraham's natural flesh and blood'.[44]

Menno, like Hofmann and Philips, holds that 'the man Christ did not have His origin on earth but in heaven.'[45] 1 Corinthians 15:47 ('The first man is from the earth, earthy; the second man is from heaven.') is explained by Menno in the following manner: 'For as the first man, Adam, is called earthy on account of his being of the earth; so, also the second man, Christ, is called heavenly because He is from heaven.'[46] Menno maintains that Christ was brought forth or begotten from 'the divine seed, material, or essence' of God the Father.[47] To Menno the matter is clear, 'Christ says that His flesh came from heaven.'[48] 'He is a heavenly fruit or man.' Indeed, the Lord Jesus did not have human flesh, but 'heavenly, innocent, obedient, blessed, and quickened flesh ....'[49]

In Menno's view the consequences of Christ's taking a human nature from Mary are devastating. The Almighty Word must have

---

41. George Williams suggests that Calvin may have come in contact with Hofmannites while in Strasbourg. Williams, p. 589.
42. Williams, p. 394.
43. Verduin, p. 793.
44. Ibid., p. 433. Cf. ibid., p. 807.
45. Ibid., p. 797.
46. Ibid., p. 798.
47. Ibid., p. 907.
48. Ibid., p. 796.
49. Ibid., pp. 437ff.

'united itself with such a little body of the flesh of Mary' and 'confined Himself.'[50] Even more disastrous is the conclusion that if Christ were born of natural, human seed, then he too partook of the 'unclean flesh of Adam' and thereby received 'the unrighteousness, curse, and sin of Adam.'[51] Thus, according to Menno, the orthodox presentation of Christ's humanity jeopardizes his redemptive work.

Calvin's case for the true humanity of Jesus Christ has Menno Simons in mind. Jesus Christ most emphatically is neither of 'heavenly seed' nor 'a phantom of a man'. He is 'a man truly begotten of human seed'. As to his humanity, Christ was 'descended from the Jews'.[52] When he is called 'Son of Man', that is a Hebrew idiom for 'a true man'. Although Christ was not immediately begotten of a mortal father, his humanity was conceived by the Holy Spirit in the virgin's womb, and 'his origin derived from Adam'.[53] The biology of Menno is simply deficient, for it is obvious that 'the woman's seed shares in the act of generation'.[54] Calvin disputes Menno's exegesis of 1 Corinthians 15:47: 'Paul is not speaking of a heavenly essence of Christ's body.' In fact, 1 Corinthians 15 in its entirety stresses Christ's true humanity, for it bases our resurrection on Christ's bodily resurrection. Christ was a real man with a human body and soul.[55]

Calvin believes that Christ's human weaknesses further demonstrated his true humanity. He was truly subject to 'the infirmities of our flesh'.[56] In the Gospel accounts 'Christ did not feign hunger,

---

50. Ibid., pp. 881, 909.
51. Ibid., p. 806. Cf. ibid., pp. 434, 846, and Williams, p. 395.
52. *Institutes* II. xiii. 1. Cf. Calvin's commentaries on Luke 1:31, Rom. 9:5, and Heb. 2:16.
53. *Institutes* II. xiii. 2. Cf. Calvin's commentaries on Dan. 7:13 and 2 Tim. 2:8.
54. *Institutes* II. xiii. 3.
55. *Institutes* II. xiii. 2. Cf. ibid., II. xvi. 12, and Calvin's commentary on John 1:14.
56. Calvin's commentary on Ps. 22:14. Cf. Calvin's commentary on Heb. 5:2.

but really felt it'.[57] He also felt a genuine thirst when he asked the Samaritan woman for a drink. When Christ stopped to rest by the well, 'he was not pretending to be tired, but was weary in very truth'.[58] Although, as to his deity, he knew all things, as to his human nature, 'his mind was subject to ignorance'.[59] Since he was 'a man subject to human needs', he needed to exercise real 'faith in God his Father'.[60]

Christ exhibited genuine human 'emotions of the soul' too.[61] Therefore 'amazement', although 'not appropriate to God ... could occur in Christ'.[62] Jesus Christ experienced real 'grief' and 'sorrow'.[63] He wept because 'He was truly endowed with human feelings'.[64] Christ knew what it was to be 'struck with fright and seized with anguish'[65] and to undergo 'the bitterest agonies of spirit' and to be 'reduced to utter extremity'.[66]

To be the Savior the eternal God became a real human being in Jesus of Nazareth. If he were not a partaker of genuine humanity, he could not save *us*. Yet Calvin steadfastly maintains that Christ's true humanity was sinless. Due to the sovereign operation of the

---

57. Calvin's commentary on Matt. 21:18.
58. Calvin's commentary on John 4:5, 7.
59. Calvin's commentary on Luke 2:40. Cf. Calvin's commentary on Matt. 24:36.
60. Calvin's commentary on Heb. 2:13.
61. Calvin's commentary on Heb. 4:15. Dominicé is correct when he writes, 'Our reformer sees in the passions of Jesus the proof and guarantee of His full humanity' (Dominicé, p. 32).
62. Calvin's commentary on Matt. 8:10.
63. *Institutes* II. xvi. 12. Cf. Calvin's commentary on Mark 8:12.
64. Calvin's commentary on Luke 19:41.
65. Calvin's commentary on Matt. 26:39. Cf. Calvin's commentary on Heb. 4:15.
66. Calvin's commentary on Heb. 5:7. For the illuminating thesis that Calvin affirmed Christ's genuine human emotions within 'proper limits,' see David L. Foxgrover, 'The Humanity of Christ: Within Proper Limits,' in *Calviniana: Ideas and Influence of John Calvin*, ed. Robert V. Schnucker, Sixteenth Century Essays & Studies, vol. 10 (Kirksville, Missouri: Sixteenth Century Journal Publishers, 1988), pp. 95-98.

Holy Spirit, the virgin birth ensured a sinless human nature for Jesus Christ. 'Christ is true man, but without fault and corruption.'[67] To be the Mediator, 'it was necessary for Him in order to cleanse others, to be clear of all uncleanness or spot.'[68] Many passages in Calvin's commentaries affirm the true and yet sinless humanity of Jesus Christ.[69]

Calvin expresses the fraternity Jesus' humanity established between Christ and the believer in many ways. Christ is 'comrade and partner in the same nature with us', so that we share a 'fellowship of nature' with him.[70] 'God's only Son put Himself on equal terms with us wishing to be our brother.'[71] We do not have to seek salvation 'at long range', but in the Lord's humanity 'it was set at the hand's reach of every man'. This is because God in Christ 'came near and opened Himself to us at close quarters'.[72] In 1 Timothy 2:5 we are told, '... there is one God and one Mediator also between God and men, the man Christ Jesus.' The Spirit of God could have said 'the God-man Christ Jesus' or 'the divine Christ Jesus', but he chose instead to say 'the *man* Christ Jesus' through the inspired writer. This was to accentuate 'the bond that unites us with God'. It is as if 'the Son of God holds out to us the hand of a brother and is joined to us by sharing our nature'.[73]

This fraternity between Christ and believers, brought about by the incarnation, is the basis for our salvation. God became *a human being for our salvation.* When Calvin first speaks of Christ's humanity in the *Institutes*, he entitles the chapter (II. xii) thus: 'Christ Had to Become Man in Order to Fulfill the Office of Mediator'. In that chapter he stresses that Christ savingly obeyed the Father in our flesh, that he won the victory over our foes in

67. *Institutes* II. xiii. 4.
68. Calvin's commentary on Luke 1:35.
69. Cf. Calvin's commentaries on Ps. 22:14, Matt. 8:3, Luke 1:35, 2:40, John 11:33, Rom. 8:3, and Heb. 4:15. Cf. *Institutes* II. xvi. 12.
70. *Institutes* II. xiii. 2.
71. Calvin's commentary on Luke 1:35.
72. Calvin's commentary on Matt. 9:6.
73. Calvin's commentary on 1 Tim. 2:5. Cf. Calvin's commentaries on 1 Tim. 3:16 and Matt. 8:3.

our flesh, and that he offered our flesh as a sacrifice to appease God's wrath.[74] Calvin carefully sets the context for his defense of Christ's true humanity in *Institutes* II. xiii. 4. At the beginning and end of that chapter he explains the purpose for which our Lord took a genuine human nature – to be our Redeemer. Calvin begins his chapter, 'It remains, then, for us to see how, clothed with our flesh, he fulfilled the office of Mediator'.[75] He concludes that important chapter with a rebuttal of the faulty inference Menno drew from Christ's true humanity. Far from being confined by his incarnation, the eternal Word of God existed totally without (*extra*) the flesh of Christ as well as totally within that flesh. Christ was a true man but did not share in the corruption of the human race. Salvation is not endangered but is ensured by Christ taking true humanity to himself. Christ's humanity was 'exempted from common corruption' because through him 'integrity was to be restored'.[76]

These beginning and concluding passages are signals indicating that Calvin affirms Christ's genuine human nature within a redemptive context. Between these signals the chapter is replete with reminders that 'the sins of the world had to be expiated in our flesh';[77] 'Christ was made man that he might make us children of God'; 'the woman's offspring is to prevail over the devil';[78] and 'Christ, the Author of salvation, was begotten of Adam, the common father of us all'.[79] Calvin's commentaries bear ample witness that he views Christ's humanity as essential for our salvation.[80]

---

74. *Institutes* II. xii. 3.
75. Ibid., II. xiii. 1.
76. Ibid., II. xiii. 4. David Foxgrover cogently argues that Calvin presents Christ's sinlessness as dynamic rather than static. 'The Humanity of Christ: Within Proper Limits,' p. 105.
77. Ibid., II. xiii. 1.
78. Ibid., II. xiii. 2.
79. Ibid., II. xiii. 3. Cf. ibid., II. xii. 3.
80. Cf. Calvin's commentaries on Rom. 8:3, 2 Cor. 13:4, Heb. 2:11, and 2:17.

God Became a Human Being *for Our Salvation*

This chapter would be incomplete without a summary of Calvin's teaching on the unity of the person of Christ. Calvin affirms the Chalcedonian position. *Institutes* II. xiv was entitled: 'How the Two Natures of the Mediator Make One Person'. The first paragraph of that chapter concludes with these words: 'For we affirm his divinity so joined and united with his humanity that each retains its distinctive nature unimpaired, and yet these two natures constitute one Christ.'[81] Calvin holds to the unity of the

---

81. *Institutes* II. xiv. 1. Wendel and others have wondered whether Calvin's accentuation of the distinction between the two natures endangers the fundamental unity of the person of Christ (François Wendel, *Calvin: Origins and Development of His Religious Thought*, p. 225). Some have written in detail of 'Nestorian tendencies' in Calvin's thought (e.g. Witte, pp. 507-15; see the reply by Hans Scholl, *Calvinus Catholicus: Die Katholische Calvinforschung Im. 20 Jahrhundert* [Freiburg: Herder, 1974], pp. 134ff., for criticism of Witte's conclusions). There is no doubt that in some places in his commentaries Calvin emphasized the distinction between the natures of Christ (Calvin's commentaries on Matt. 8:23-25, 14:14, 15:21, and Mark 7:24-30). In many other places, however, he teaches the unity of Christ's person (Calvin's commentaries on Luke 1:43, John 1:14, Acts 20:28, Gal. 4:4, and Phil. 2:7, 10). His orthodoxy with respect to the unity of natures in Christ has been ably defended (see Willis, pp. 62ff., Marvin P. Hoogland, 'Calvin's Perspective on the Exaltation of Christ in Comparison with the Post-Reformation Doctrine of the Two States,' p. 209, and Dominicé, pp. 43f.). Berkouwer's comments are especially apt when he shows that the same criticisms directed against Calvin were levelled at Chalcedon itself (G. C. Berkouwer, *The Person of Christ*, Studies in Dogmatics [Grand Rapids: Eerdmans, 1954], pp. 286f.). I agree with those who acknowledge the problematic passages in the commentaries and yet see these in the light of Calvin's overall thought and conclude in favor of his Chalcedonian orthodoxy.

Calvin's theological development as a result of his polemics with Francisco Stancaro is significant in a discussion of his view of the unity of Christ's person (for historical background see Joseph N. Tylenda, 'Christ the Mediator: Calvin versus Stancaro', *Calvin Theological Journal*

two natures in the person of Christ – God really became a human being. Calvin's perspective is lost unless it is immediately added – *for our salvation*. He writes, 'Divinity and humanity are the two requisites which we must look for in Christ if we are to find salvation in Him. His divinity contains power, righteousness, and life, which are communicated to us by His humanity.'[82]

The incarnation is Calvin's prerequisite for the atonement. He taught the true deity, humanity, and unity of the person of Christ in relation to the redemptive goal of the incarnation. God became a human being *for our salvation*. To lose sight of this when

---

8 [1973]: 5-11, and Joseph N. Tylenda, 'The Controversy on Christ the Mediator: Calvin's Second Reply to Stancaro', *Calvin Theological Journal* 8 [1973]: 131-44). Stancaro, who claimed that Christ was Mediator only in regard to His human nature, caused Calvin more strongly to affirm the unity of Christ's person. In Calvin's first letter to Stancaro he writes, 'It is also true to say that all the actions which Christ performed to reconcile God and man refer to the whole person, and are not to be separately restricted to only one nature' (Tylenda, 'Christ the Mediator', pp. 14f.).

Another factor that buttresses the contention that Calvin stood in the line of Chalcedonian orthodoxy is his employment of the *communicatio idiomatum*. Witte has criticized Calvin for having no real interest in the communication of attributes and for not founding this interchange on an ontological union of the two natures in Christ, but on His mediatorial office (Witte, pp. 503ff.). Willis and Tylenda have rightly taken issue with Witte's remarks (Willis, pp. 66f., and Joseph N. Tylenda, 'Calvin's Understanding of the Communication of Properties', *The Westminster Theological Journal* 38 [1975-76]: 54-65). Tylenda has demonstrated that in Calvin's use of the *communicatio idiomatum* 'the subject of predication must be taken in the concrete and not in the abstract'. Hence in the communication of properties 'an attribute of one nature is assigned to the person of Christ, though designated by his other nature' (Tylenda, 'Calvin's Understanding', pp. 62-65). As a result 'Calvin's use of the *communicatio idiomatum* strengthens rather than weakens his affirmation of the unity of the person of Jesus Christ' (Willis, p. 59). Cf. Calvin's commentary on Acts 20:28 and *Institutes* II. xiv. 2.

82. Calvin's commentary on Rom. 1:3.

discussing Calvin's Christology is to misrepresent his thought.[83] Two discussions highlight the soteriological thrust of Calvin's doctrine of Christ. The first is his battle with Osiander over the motive for the incarnation. The second is his doctrine of Christ as Mediator.

Osiander maintains that 'Christ would still have become man even if no means of redeeming mankind had been needed'.[84] Christ would in this way have shown his love for his unfallen people. To say that God's plan to send the Redeemer depended upon the fall limits God in Osiander's eyes. Scripture never denies that Christ would have become man apart from the fall; it is therefore presumptuous for us to do so.[85] Angels and the church would have lacked their Head if God did not become incarnate in Christ.[86] Man and woman were made in God's image according to the pattern of Christ to come. God made Adam and Eve like Christ, whom God had already determined was to become incarnate.[87]

Calvin's answers to these arguments of Osiander are given in *Institutes* II. xii, where he argues that Osiander's whole contention is useless speculation, beyond the witness of Scripture. Scripture always links the incarnation and redemption. To sever them is not only speculative, but dangerous.[88]

---

83. Trevor Hart's summary deserves quotation: 'As far as christology is concerned Calvin places himself firmly within the tradition of Chalcedonian orthodoxy, both in the letter and the spirit. Furthermore, the pattern of his christology is determinative for his soteriology.... Who Christ is makes all the difference for interpreting the significance of what he does.' 'Humankind in Christ and Christ in Humankind: Salvation as Participation in Our Substitute in the Theology of John Calvin,' *Scottish Journal of Theology* 42 (1989): 71.
84. *Institutes* II. xii. 4. Calvin here cites arguments set forth by Osiander in his treatise, *An filius Dei incarnandus* (1550).
85. *Institutes* II. xii. 5.
86. Ibid., II. xii. 7.
87. Ibid., II. xii. 6.
88. Ibid., II. xii. 4.

Calvin addresses Osiander's contention that, if redemption is the reason for the incarnation, God is limited because his plan is made dependent upon the fall. Osiander is guilty of 'impious boldness' by seeking to know more than God has ordained by his secret decree. To say, as Osiander does, that Scripture never denies that God would have become incarnate apart from the fall, and that we should not deny it either, is for Calvin a *reductio ad absurdum*. One could thus 'prove' all sorts of perverse things nowhere explicitly denied in the Bible. No, that would never do. Positive proof is demanding for so important a matter.[89] As for angels or believers lacking a Head unless the Son of God became incarnate, again Osiander errs. Christ was the Head of angels prior to the incarnation. If there had been no fall, he could have been the Head of the church in the same way.[90] Osiander's argument from the image of God is more idle speculation. Calvin replies that Christ was the image of God before he became a man.[91]

More important than Calvin's detailed answers to Osiander's arguments is his basic response to them. 'All Scripture proclaims that to become our Redeemer he was clothed with flesh.' That closes the matter for Calvin. To inquire further is perverse speculation – speculation because it transgresses the limits God set in his Word, and perverse because it insults the God who gave the Scriptures and who sent his Son to be the Savior of the world. Calvin marshals an impressive array of scriptural testimonies to demonstrate his contention that salvation was the motive of the incarnation.[92] The very title of *Institutes* II. xii summarizes Calvin's position: 'Christ Had to Become Man in Order to Fulfill the Office of Mediator'.

'This controversy is significant, for it tended to ground Calvin's Christology on Soteriology.'[93] The two were inseparably united

---

89. Ibid., II. xii. 5. 90. Ibid., II. xii. 7.
91. Ibid., II. xii. 6. 92. Ibid., II. xii. 4.
93. Justo L. González, *A History of Christian Thought*, vol. 3, *From the Protestant Reformation to the Twentieth Century* (Nashville: Abingdon, 1975), p. 136.

by Calvin's insistence that redemption was the motive for Jesus' incarnation. Notwithstanding his strong convictions on predestination, Calvin does not reason from God's decrees to the ideas of Osiander. Calvin devotes himself not to speculative abstractions but to faithful biblical exposition.[94] For him, 'Christ does not exist apart from His work, nor has His work any meaning apart from the fact that it is His work.'[95] Calvin's commentaries make the same point:

> And indeed, faith should not cling only to the essence of Christ, so to say, but should pay heed to His power and office. For it would be of little advantage to know who Christ is unless the second point is added of what He wishes to be towards us and for what purpose He was sent by the Father.[96]

Calvin's favorite way of saying 'the person and work of Christ' is simply to speak of the 'Mediator': 'Now it was of the greatest importance for us that he who was to be our Mediator be both true God and true man.' The human race suffers from a double plight. Our finitude separates us from God. 'Even if man had remained free from all stain, his condition would have been too lowly for him to reach God without a Mediator.' An even greater gulf between God and ourselves is fixed because of our sinfulness. 'What then, of man: plunged by his moral ruin into death and hell, defiled with so many spots, befouled with his own corruption, and overwhelmed with every curse?' Only as God is Jesus able to help us, and only as man is he near enough to touch us in our deepest weakness. The Mediator, therefore, must be both God and man.[97]

The work of the Mediator is already foretold by the Old

94. G. C. Berkouwer, *The Work of Christ*, p. 27.

95. Paul Van Buren, *Christ in Our Place: the Substitutionary Character of Calvin's Doctrine of Reconciliation*, p. 141.

96. Calvin's commentary on John 1:49. Cf. Calvin's commentaries on Matt. 1:16, 21, 2:4, and Luke 1:31.

97. *Institutes* II. xii. 1. Cf. Calvin's commentary on 1 Pet. 1:21 for a statement of humanity's double plight of finitude and sin.

Testament prophets when they 'set forth Christ as the Mediator, who is to propitiate God for us by procuring forgiveness for our sins.'[98] Because he is 'the Mediator of reconciliation, by whom we are accepted of God,' he is also 'the Mediator of intercession, through whom the way is opened for us to call upon the Father.' Furthermore, Christ 'has always been the Mediator of all teaching, because by Him God has always revealed Himself to men.'[99] We should emphasize the word *always*. Even before the incarnation, Christ was 'the perpetual Mediator' who was 'always the bond of communication between God and man ... because God formally manifested Himself in no other way than through Him.'[100] Thus in his exposition of Jacob's ladder, Calvin writes, 'the ladder is a figure of Christ' as 'the only Mediator who reaches from heaven down to earth.'[101] The Old Testament believers knew God only through the Mediator. There is no knowledge of God apart from his revelation in Christ. The Lord Jesus is Mediator of the Old Testament, as well as the New.[102]

---

98. Calvin's commentary on Acts 10:43.
99. Calvin's commentary on Gal. 3:19.
100. Calvin's commentary on Gen. 48:16.
101. Calvin's commentary on Gen. 28:12.
102. *Institutes* II. x. Cf. Calvin's commentary on Acts 7:30. Willis notes an important development in Calvin's doctrine of Christ the Mediator: 'Calvin's deployment of the term "Mediator" undergoes decisive change as he is forced to clarify his own position in response to the doctrine of Francisco Stancaro' (Willis, pp. 69ff.). Stancaro maintains that 1 Tim. 2:5 could only be understood as teaching that Christ was Mediator solely with reference to His Human nature. Calvin counters this doctrine by affirming that Christ is Mediator in both natures. Calvin is pushed by Stancaro to label Christ Mediator in His role of eternal sustainer of the world. Although this role has been ascribed to the eternal Word by writers from the patristic period on, Calvin sets theological precedent by applying the term 'Mediator' to this preincarnate work of Christ. The concept of Christ as Mediator prior to the incarnation is really a corollary to Calvin's affirmation that Christ is Mediator in both divine and human natures after the incarnation. Since the incarnate Christ is Mediator according to His deity (and humanity), He must have been

Calvin's comments on 1 John 4:2 ('By this you know the Spirit of God: every spirit that confesses that Jesus Christ has come in the flesh is from God') form a fitting conclusion to this chapter:

> But let us remember what this confession contains. When the apostle says that Christ came, we infer that He was before with the Father. By this His eternal divinity is shown. By saying that He came in the flesh, he means that by putting on flesh, He became a real man, of the same nature with us, that He became our brother – except that He was free from all sin and corruption. And finally, by saying that He came we must note the cause of His coming; for the Father did not send Him for nothing. Christ's office and power depend on this.[103]

Mediator even prior to the incarnation as eternal Son of God. Calvin's contest with Stancaro leads him to make more emphatic statements that the Mediator's work of reconciliation was accomplished in both natures. Calvin says: 'It is also true to say that all the actions which Christ performed to reconcile God and man refer to the whole person and are not to be separately restricted to only one nature', and 'We will not separate the natures in the act of dying, since Atonement could not have been effected by man alone unless the divine power were conjoined' (Tylenda, 'Christ the Mediator', pp. 14f.).

103. Calvin's commentary on 1 John 4:2.

3

CHRIST'S THREEFOLD OFFICE OF PROPHET, KING, AND PRIEST

'To know the purpose for which Christ was sent by the Father, and what he conferred upon us, we must look above all at three things in Him: the prophetic office, kingship, and priesthood' (*Inst.* II. xv, title).

There are two chief ways in which John Calvin explains the meaning of the saving work of Christ: by using six biblical themes of the atonement, and by employing the concept of Christ's threefold messianic office of prophet, king, and priest. Chapters 4 through 9 will treat Calvin's themes of the work of Christ. We will now examine his presentation of Christ's work in terms of the threefold office or *munus triplex*.

The concept of 'office' to describe Christ's saving activity has a long history. In the patristic period both the twofold office (Christ as king and priest) and the threefold office (Christ as prophet, king and priest) occur.[1] Calvin's writings show a movement from the use of the *munus duplex* (twofold office) to that of the *munus triplex*. He employs the twofold office idea in the first (1536) edition of the *Institutes*. In his treatise 'Instruction in Faith' of 1537, the twofold office appears again. In the 1539 *Institutes* the prophetic office occurs for the first time, but it is not yet directly related to the title 'Christ'. In the Geneva Catechism (1541),[2] the 1545 *Institutes*, the Catechism of 1543, and the final

---

1. John F. Jansen, *Calvin's Doctrine of the Work of Christ* (London: J. Clarke, 1956), pp. 26-38.
2. So Jonathan Tice, 'The Structure and Evolution of Calvin's Doctrine of the Atonement,' in *Church Divinity*, ed. John Henry Morgan. Church Divinity Monograph Series (Bristol: Wyndham Hall Press, 1991), 76-77.

(1559) edition of the *Institutes*, the threefold office appears as Calvin's exposition of the messianic name.[3]

---

3. Ibid., pp. 39-44. When scholars have attempted to interpret this evidence, two different views have emerged. Jansen argues for a rejection of the prophetic office in Calvin. Others have held that Calvin's presentation of the *munus triplex* in the 1559 *Institutes* was a mature reflection of his theological thought. Jansen contends that Calvin's movement from a twofold to a threefold messianic office was merely 'peripheral' and 'an artificial change'. In fact, 'it is not an adequate or true expression of his own theology' (ibid., pp. 51, 105f.). Calvin arrived at the *munus triplex* because of his desire for systematization. His motive was to safeguard the ministerial order (ibid., pp. 45-51). Jansen finds further corroboration of his thesis in the fact that 'the triple formula never appears in his commentaries .... Calvin the exegete refuses to follow Calvin the systematizer' (ibid., pp. 74f.). Timothy P. Palmer follows Jansen in defending a twofold messianic office in Calvin ('John Calvin's View of the Kingdom of God', Ph.D. diss., [Aberdeen: University of Aberdeen, 1988] p. 137).

It is undeniable that the *munus duplex* is employed in Calvin's biblical exegesis (cf. Calvin's commentaries on Ps. 110:4, Zech. 6:11, Luke 2:25, and Acts 10:38). Yet I must reject Jansen's thesis of an inoperative prophetic office in Calvin. I concur with E. David Willis, who wrote, 'the prophetic office is much more integral to Calvin's thought than J. F. Jansen admits it to be' (E. David Willis, *Calvin's Catholic Christology*, p.86 n. 1). Milner (Benjamin Charles Milner, *Calvin's Doctrine of the Church*, Studies in the History of Christian Thought, vol. 5 [Leiden: Brill, 1970] p. 164n.) and G. C. Berkouwer (*The Work of Christ*, pp. 61f.) are likewise constrained to reject Jansen's main thesis. The prophetic office of Christ plays an important role in both Calvin's *Institutes* and his commentaries. The place afforded to Christ's prophetic office in the 1559 *Institutes* must be given due weight. The title of II. xv ('To Know the Purpose for Which Christ Was Sent by the Father, and What He conferred Upon Us, We Must Look Above All at Three Things in Him: the Prophetic Office, Kingship, and Priesthood') shows the importance of all three aspects of Christ's messianic office. At various places in the chapter Calvin affirms the importance of the prophetic office as well as the other two offices (cf. II. xv. 1, 2). Contrary to Jansen's contention, Calvin's commentaries do demonstrate that the *munus triplex*

The Prophetic Office of Christ

Christ in his office of prophet was a teacher of doctrine during his earthly ministry. In the *Institutes*, Calvin tells how God gave the Old Testament people 'an unbroken line of prophets' who brought them 'useful doctrine sufficient for salvation'. Yet these prophets pointed to the great messianic teacher who was to come. They hoped for 'the full light of understanding only at the coming of the Messiah.'[4] In his commentary on Luke, Calvin writes, 'No-one was ever a more gifted or suitable Teacher of the Gospel than the Lord Himself.'[5] Jesus Christ did not bring abstract doctrine, but teaching that was intimately connected with his person. He was the center of the Good News; he was the Savior of the world.[6]

Christ as a teacher of the Word of God bears 'the perfection of the gospel doctrine.'[7] This notion of the perfection of Christ's

---

functions in Calvin's biblical exegesis. In some passages Calvin links Christ's anointing as Messiah with His prophetic office (cf. Calvin's commentaries on Isa. 61:1, Luke 4:18, and John 4:25f.). In some places a *munus duplex* is said to consist of Christ as prophet and king (Calvin's commentary on Ps. 2:7) or as prophet and priest (Calvin's commentary on Heb. 4:14). This shows the importance of the prophetic office in Calvin's thinking. In other places he employs a *munus triplex* of prophet, king, and priest to summarize Christ's redemptive activity (Calvin's commentaries on Matt. 21:12 and John 17:4). I am compelled by such evidence to side with the majority of Calvin scholars who regard the threefold messianic office of Christ as an important element in Calvin's theology. I agree with Randall C. Zachman: 'Far from being tangential to Calvin's thought, the prophetic office of Christ is foundational to books 3 and 4 of the 1559 Institutes,' 'Jesus Christ as the Image of God in Calvin's Theology,' *Calvin Theological Journal* 25 (1990): 54, n. 14.

4. *Institutes* II. xv. 1.

5. Calvin's commentary on Luke 24:27.

6. Klauspeter Blaser, *Calvins Lehre von den drei Ämtern Christi*, Theologische Studien, vol. 105 (Zürich: EVZ-Verlag, 1970), p. 12. Cf. Joachim Staedtke, 'Die Lehre von der Königsherrschaft Christi und den zwei Reichen bei Calvin', *Kerygma und Dogma* (1972), 18:205.

7. *Institutes* II. xv. 1.

teaching occurs in the *Institutes*: 'And the prophetic dignity in Christ leads us to know that in the sum of doctrine as he has given it to us all parts of perfect wisdom are contained.'[8]

Calvin's commentaries make the same point. Since Christ is 'the highest and unique Doctor of His church',[9] Christians obtain 'absolute perfection of wisdom in Him.'[10]

Because Jesus Christ brought the perfection of doctrine, he brought also 'the fullness and culmination of all revelations.'[11] This must be viewed from a perspective of the whole Bible, Old and New Testaments. Calvin remarks in his commentary on John, 'Yet we know that, inasmuch as He is the eternal Wisdom of God, He is the only fount of all doctrine and that all the prophets who have been from the beginning spoke by His Spirit.'[12]

God revealed himself to his Old Testament people Israel; yet this revelation was in shadows, in partial form through the prophets. Now Christians enjoy perfect light because the reality to which the shadows pointed is here – Christ himself. God's revelation is no longer incomplete, for we have 'the full and perfect manifestation of all things.'[13] Now the great prophet has come, endowed with the prophetic office by the anointing of the Holy Spirit, and he has given us 'the perfect doctrine'. As such he 'has made an end to all prophecies'.[14] It was for this reason

---

8. Ibid., II. xv. 2.

9. Calvin's commentary on Matt. 17:5. Cf. Calvin's commentary on Heb. 2:13.

10. Calvin's commentary on 1 Cor. 1:30. Cf. Calvin's commentary on John 14:10.

11. *Institutes* II. xv. 1.

12. Calvin's commentary on John 14:24.

13. Calvin's commentary on Acts 3:22.

14. *Institutes* II. xv. 2. Blaser correctly insists that we read II. xv in the light of II. ix-xi (especially chapter ix). The prophetic office must be viewed in the context of 'promise and fulfillment, of law and gospel, of the prophetic and the present'. As a prophet Christ is the 'full manifestation of God'. Hence 'the prophetic office as the office of the Word forms the relation between the two Testaments and guarantees the unity of Scripture' (Blaser, pp. 27f.).

Calvin entitles *Institutes* I. ix, 'Fanatics, Abandoning Scripture and Flying Over to Revelation, Cast Down All the Principles of Godliness.' Christ is the end of prophetic revelation from God. Anabaptists who claim to receive direct revelations from God are abandoning Scripture. They stumble because they do not understand the practical consequences of Christ's execution of his prophetic office – we are to expect no fresh revelations from God.

God continues to speak, however, by the Holy Spirit through his written Word. Christ as prophet continues to teach by his Spirit through his ministers. In this way Christ in heaven continues his prophetic ministry begun on earth. Jesus Christ

> received anointing, not only for himself, that he might carry out the office of teaching, but for his whole body that the power of the Spirit might be present in the continuing preaching of the gospel .... This anointing was diffused from the Head to the members ....[15]

Calvin places emphasis on the present ministry of the Spirit of God. It is because the Holy Spirit is the Spirit of Christ that the Mediator exercises his heavenly prophetic ministry. Weier sums up the matter well when he writes, 'The effusion of the Spirit is thus Christologically grounded and is the completion of the prophetic office of Christ.'[16]

A word should be said about the ministers through whom Christ performs his present prophetic ministry by the Spirit. Jesus Christ is 'the Pastor who feeds His flock by teaching and to whom the teaching office is exclusive.' His ministers function 'always as instruments of His unique teaching office'; for Christ is the 'sovereign and unique teacher of His church'.[17] It is on this basis

---

15. *Institutes* II. xv. 2.
16. Boniface A. Willems and Reinhold Weier, *Soteriologie von der Reformation bis zur Gegenwart*, Handbuch der Dogmengeschichte, vol. 3, fasc. 2c (Freiburg: Herder, 1972), p. 29.
17. Alexandre Ganoczy, *Calvin: Théologien de L'église et du ministère*, Unam Sanctam (Paris: Les Éditions du Cerf, 1964), 48:178.

that Calvin warns preachers of the Word: 'The teachers set over the Church are not to put forward whatever they may think, but must themselves depend solely on the mouth of one Teacher ....'[18]

The distinction between Christ as prophet during his earthly ministry and as present heavenly prophet does not mean a dichotomy of the Spirit's role. The Holy Spirit was present in Christ's earthly prophetic ministry, even as he was later sent by the Father and Son in a special way to continue that work. On earth Christ was both outer and inner teacher. Calvin comments on Luke 24:32: 'Christ alone enjoys both properties, of speaking a word outwardly, and effectively shaping the heart to the obedience of faith.'[19] This 'inner' teaching is accomplished by Christ through the Holy Spirit. In his exposition of Romans 8:15, Calvin says: 'Paul is making a deliberate contrast because of false apostles between the literal disciples of the law and believers, whom Christ, their heavenly Master not only addresses with the words of His mouth, but also teaches inwardly and effectively by His Spirit.'[20] This theme of Christ as outer and inner teacher is found in many places in Calvin's commentaries.[21] The notion of outer and inner teacher is important, for it ties Christ's prophetic office to redemption.[22] Christ's preaching was redemptive because, as Calvin explains in his commentary on Luke 4:17, 'He was endowed with the fullness of the Spirit, to be a witness and ambassador for our reconciliation with God ....' Jesus 'alone, by the power of His Spirit, effects and provides the benefits promised here.'[23]

---

18. Calvin's commentary on Matt. 28:20.
19. Calvin's commentary on Luke 24:32.
20. Calvin's commentary on Rom. 8:15.
21. See Calvin's commentaries on Matt. 15:23, Luke 24:17, 45, and John 5:25.
22. As Parker aptly wrote, 'His preaching was a part of His redemptive activity – as necessary a part as His "offices" of priest and king' (T. H. L. Parker, *Calvin's Doctrine of the Knowledge of God*, rev. ed. [Grand Rapids: Eerdmans, 1959], pp. 81f.).
23. It is this connection between Christ's prophetic office and his work

Christ as prophet in his earthly ministry and Christ as heavenly prophet today teaches doctrine by his Spirit's working in the hearts of men and women. The center of that doctrine is the gospel – the Good News that Jesus Christ died for sinners. It was the concern of Calvin to affirm that the application of the gospel to sinner's hearts is a redemptive work performed by the great and final prophet, the Lord Jesus Christ, through his Spirit.

The Kingly Office of Christ

'Christ was anointed as king by the Holy Spirit.'[24] In fact, Calvin teaches that 'Christ was called Messiah especially with respect to, and by virtue of, his kingship.'[25] What is the nature of his reign? Calvin has one answer to this question – Christ's kingship 'is spiritual in nature'. From the spiritual nature of Christ's reign Calvin infers 'its efficacy and benefit, as well as its whole force and eternity.'[26] In the *Institutes* he writes, 'For since it is not earthly or carnal and hence subject to corruption, but spiritual, it lifts us up even to eternal life.'[27] When did this spiritual reign of Christ begin? Although in a sense it began when Christ was still on earth (his resurrection especially displayed 'His glory and power'), 'yet He truly inaugurated His kingdom only at His ascension into heaven.' Even more specifically, it is Christ's session at the Father's right hand that marks the time 'that Christ

---

of salvation that Jansen could not see. Jansen would have profited from Schellong's observation that in Bucer's and Oecolampadius' writings 'the relation of the teaching office of Christ to the office of redemption was unclear, so it must be, as long as Christ's teaching is understood only as external teaching office' (Dieter Schellong, *Calvins Auslegung der synoptischen Evangelien*, pp. 270f.). But as Schellong demonstrates, and as Jansen failed to take into account, when Calvin in the 1559 *Institutes* presents Christ's prophetic office, he accentuates his role as inner teacher.

24. *Institutes* II. xv. 5.

25. Ibid., II. xv. 2.

26. Ibid., II. xv. 3. Cf. ibid., III. xxv. 5 for Calvin's vigorous denunciation of chiliasm.

27. Ibid., II. xv. 4.

was invested with lordship over heaven and earth, and solemnly entered into possession of the government committed to Him.'[28] The full and outward manifestation of Christ's kingship is eschatological and will take place at his second coming.[29]

The redemptive force of Christ's royal office is shown by the fact that for the sake of his people he was anointed king by the Holy Spirit. Calvin explains, 'Christ enriches his people with all things necessary for the eternal salvation of souls.'[30] Jesus Christ gives of his Holy Spirit to believers to help them in their spiritual need. Christians receive eternal life itself from the Spirit sent from their king, Jesus Christ. In the *Institutes* Calvin says:

> For it is only in this way that we are invigorated. Especially with regard to heavenly life, there is no drop of vigor in us save what the Holy Spirit instills. For the Spirit has chosen Christ as His seat, that from Him might abundantly flow the heavenly riches of which we are in such need. The believers stand unconquered through the strength of their king, and His spiritual riches abound in them. Hence they are justly called Christians.[31]

The benefits of Christ's spiritual reign extend to the whole body of the church, and to each member. The king is the 'eternal protector and defender of His church.' In his kingly role Christ 'assures the godly of the everlasting preservation of the church' so that 'amid the violent agitation with which it is continually troubled, amid the grievous and frightful storms that threaten it with unnumbered calamities, it still remains safe.' God's people must arm themselves with the knowledge that 'the perpetuity of the church is secure in this protection.'[32] Thus, the fact that

---

28. Ibid., II. xvi. 14.
29. Calvin's commentary on Matt. 25:31. Cf. *Institutes* II. xv. 5, where Calvin maintains that the last judgment will be the final act of Christ's reign. Cf. Blaser, pp. 16f.
30. *Institutes* II. xv. 4.
31. Ibid., II. xv. 5. Cf. Tjarko Stadtland, *Rechtfertigung und Heiligung bei Calvin*, p. 143.
32. *Institutes* II. xv. 3.

Christians persevere in the faith is due to Christ's exercise of his royal office on their behalf. When believers fear falling away, they can be confident knowing:

> The Father has given all power to the Son that He may by the Son's hand govern, nourish, and sustain us, keep us in His care, and help us. Thus, while for the short time we wander away from God, Christ stands in our midst, to lead us little by little to a firm union with God.[33]

Calvin's doctrine of the Christian life urges the believer to press on, struggling against sin. The Christian is called to self-denial, by bearing the cross.[34] In the midst of this life of hardship and struggle, there is spiritual victory. This victory is possible because of the ministry of Christ the king on behalf of his people. Jesus 'fortifies' Christians 'with courage to stand unconquerable against all the assaults of spiritual enemies.' Calvin reminds believers that on account of Christ's spiritual reign 'let us not doubt that we shall always be victorious over the devil, the world, and every kind of harmful thing.' Although the Christian's lot is hard, 'Our king will never leave us destitute, but will provide for our needs ... and also provide us with confidence to struggle fearlessly against the devil, sin, and death.'[35] Unfortunately, this accent of victory in Calvin's doctrine of the Christian life has gone too often unnoticed.

There are corporate protection and victory for the church. And there is also individual blessing for Christians derived from Christ's kingly office, as Calvin explains in the *Institutes*:

> Now with regard to the special application of this to each of us – the same 'eternity' ought to inspire us to hope for blessed immortality .... Therefore Christ, to lift our hope to heaven, declares that His 'kingship is not of this world' (John 18:36). In short, when any one of us hears that Christ's kingship is spiritual, aroused by this word

---

33. Ibid., II. xv. 5.
34. Ibid., II. vii, viii.
35. Ibid., II. xv. 4.

> let him attain to the hope of a better life; and since it is now protected by God's hand, let him await the full fruit of this grace in the age to come.[36]

The Priestly Office of Christ

I have followed Calvin's ordering of the *munus triplex* (prophet, king, and priest) as found in *Institutes* II. xv rather than the traditional post-Reformation Reformed order of prophet, priest, and king. The priestly office, like the other two, must be viewed from an Old Testament perspective. Equally important for understanding Calvin's exposition of the high priestly office of Christ is his Hebrews commentary.[37] The burden of the letter to the Hebrews is to show how Christ is the complete fulfillment of Old Testament predictions and types, how he is 'better' than his Old Testament foreshadows. Calvin, referring to Hebrews 7:1-10, writes in his commentary on Mark, 'When Christ, the true Melchizedek and the eternal priest, was brought to light there had to be fulfilled in Him what was foreshadowed in the figures of the law.'[38]

Christ's priestly office must be understood in the light of Old Testament prediction and New Testament fulfillment. Yet, it is only in terms of its Old Testament background that the uniqueness of Christ's priesthood stands out. Jesus and his work constitute the reality of which their Old Testament antecedents were only shadows. In Christ 'the priesthood and the ceremonies of the Old Covenant have come to their end.'[39] This statement has both

---

36. Ibid., II. xv. 3.
37. See Stadtland, p. 141. As Staedtke has aptly summarized, 'In *Institutes* II. xv, xvi, Calvin has interpreted the high priestly office entirely in the sense of Heb. 7 and 8-10' (Staedtke, 'Königsherrschaft', p. 205).
38. Calvin's commentary on Mark 16:19.
39. Schellong, *Calvins Auslegung der synoptischen Evangelien*, p. 262. Cf. Calvin's exposition of the rending of the temple curtain in his commentary on Matt. 27:51. Wolf (Hans H. Wolf, *Die Einheit des Bundes: Das Verhältnis von Altem und Neuem Testament bei Calvin*, 2nd ed.

positive and negative sides. Positively, Christ is the end, the fulfillment and completion of the Old Testament cultus. Negatively, he is the end of the same. There is, then, no more validity to Old Testament rites.

Our Lord's uniqueness as high priest over the house of God is further demonstrated by his union of divine and human natures. As Calvin expressed in his first letter to Stancaro, 'This divinity is a necessary requisite of the office of Priesthood.'[40] God's great high priest had to be divine; he also had to be genuinely human, as Calvin explains in his commentary on Hebrews 5:2:

> He says that the priests are taken from among men. Hence it follows that Christ must have been truly man. Because we stand a long way off from God, we are in some way placed before Him in His priestly character. This could not be so if He were not one of us. The fact that the Son of Man has a common nature with us does not detract

---

[Neukirchen: Erziehungsverein, 1958], p. 155) has done an excellent job of summarizing the uniqueness of Christ in the light of Old Testament priests and priesthood:

1. The Old Testament priesthood is *temporalis figura*; Christ's is perpetual.
2. Old Testament priests must succeed one another; Christ is a perpetual priest.
3. Christ's deity is without beginning according to the order of Melchizedek.
4. Whereas under the law priesthood and kingship are separate, with Christ these are joined.
5. The Old Testament priests are copies; Christ is the truth.
6. Priests must pray for their own forgiveness; Christ stands in complete righteousness before God.
7. The priestly dignity was derived from outer garments, but Christ bears the dignity in Himself.
8. Priests expiated sins with the blood of beasts; Christ expiated sins with His own blood.

Cf. Calvin's commentary on Heb. 7:16f., 26.

40. Joseph N. Tylenda, 'Christ the Mediator', p. 14. Cf. Tylenda, 'The Controversy on Christ the Mediator', p. 149, and Ganoczy, p. 165.

> from His dignity, but rather commends Him the more to us. He is fitted to reconcile God to us because He is man.[41]

Christ's priesthood is unique because, of all priests, he is the only one to be both priest and sacrifice for sin. Calvin explains:

> Although God under the law commanded animal sacrifices to be offered to himself, in Christ there was a new and different order, in which the same one was to be both priest and sacrifice. This was because no other satisfaction adequate for our sins, and no other man worthy to offer to God the only-begotten Son, could be found.[42]

The concept of Christ as priest and sacrifice highlights the unity of Christ's person and work in Calvin's theology.[43] Christ's death on the cross was his ultimate consecration into priestly service. In his commentary on Hebrews 5:9, Calvin says:

> The final and so-called remoter purpose why Christ had to suffer was that in this way He was initiated into His priesthood. It is as if the apostle were saying that to endure the Cross and to die were a solemn form of consecration for Christ thus indicating that all His sufferings had regard to our salvation.[44]

The union of the Mediator's person and work in which Christ is both priest and sacrifice has importance for redemption: 'The case of Christ is quite different. He needed no sacrifice inasmuch as He was not tainted by any stain of sin. His sacrifice was such that its once-for-all oblation sufficed to the end of the world. He offered Himself.'[45] Christ, the spotless Son of God, offered up

---

41. Cf. Paul Van Buren, *Christ in Our Place*, p. 67, and Willis, p. 90.
42. *Institutes* II. xv. 6.
43. Blaser (pp. 40f.) correctly points this out.
44. See Ronald S. Wallace, *Calvin's Doctrine of the Christian Life* (Grand Rapids: Eerdmans, 1959), pp. 6-8, for a fuller discussion of Christ's consecration to priesthood.
45. Calvin's commentary on Heb. 7:27. Van Buren stresses the substitutionary aspects of Christ as priest and sacrifice: 'But the real

himself as the final sacrifice for sin. It is precisely in this connection that Calvin so vehemently attacks the Roman Catholic mass: 'The more detestable is the fabrication of those, who not content with Christ's priesthood, have presumed to sacrifice him anew! The papists attempt this each day, considering the mass as the sacrificing of Christ.'[46]

Calvin carefully distinguishes the two purposes of Christ's priestly office: reconciliation and intercession:

> Now, Christ plays the priestly role, not only to render the Father favorable and propitious towards us by an eternal law of reconciliation, but also to receive us as his companions in this great office (Rev. 1:6). For we who are defiled in ourselves, yet are priests in him ....[47]

In both Old and New Testament commentaries Calvin likewise combines the two parts of Christ's priestly office.[48]

Salvation depends upon Christ's high priestly work of reconciliation. Calvin employs a variety of biblical words and themes to express this. Christ's priestly work is to reconcile us to God, to appease God's wrath by propitiation, to present a sacrifice with his blood to blot out our guilt, to make satisfaction for our sins, and to obtain grace for us and give us access to God.[49]

The second of Christ's priestly duties is intercession. Because Jesus Christ has reconciled the Father to believers and them to him, he has opened for them a way of access to God in prayer. In the *Institutes* Calvin explains that Christ's accomplishment of reconciliation is the prerequisite for his work of intercession:

---

emphasis on substitution comes in the consideration of the sacrificial victim, for the victim was nothing other than a substitute, under the laws of sacrifice .... Simply to speak of Christ as priest, therefore, is meaningless, if we do not see that He was a priest only in so far as He offered up a sacrifice for our sins' (Van Buren, p. 70).

46. *Institutes* II. xv. 6.

47. Ibid.

48. See Calvin's commentaries on Isa. 53:12 and 1 Tim. 2:6.

49. *Institutes* II. xv. 6.

> For, having entered a sanctuary not made with hands, He appears before the Father's face as our constant advocate and intercessor (Heb. 7:25; 9:11f.; Rom. 8:34). Thus He turns the Father's eyes to His own righteousness to avert His gaze from our sins. He so reconciles the Father's heart to us by His intercession that He prepares a way and access for us to the Father's throne. He fills with grace and kindness the throne that for miserable sinners would otherwise have been filled with dread.[50]

In fact, according to Calvin's commentary on 1 John 2:1, 'Christ's intercession is the continual application of His death to our salvation.'[51] Christ's priestly work of reconciliation is once for all. But his high priestly function of intercession is continuous. He continually intercedes on behalf of his people before his Father's throne.[52]

Great benefits accrue to believers because of Christ's ministry of intercession. Christians can enjoy peace of conscience knowing that God has fully accepted them in Jesus Christ and that Christ continuously pleads their case before the Father. Another benefit is access to God in prayer. Calvin's statements on the priesthood of believers, a favorite theme of Luther, are rare. Calvin pens the following:

> Christ acted to receive us as his companions in this great office (Rev. 1:6). For we who are defiled in ourselves, yet are priests in him, offer ourselves and our all to God, and freely enter the heavenly sanctuary that the sacrifices of prayers and praise that we bring may be acceptable and sweet smelling before God.[53]

---

50. Ibid., II. xvi. 16.
51. Hoogland expresses this very well: 'The intercession of Christ according to Calvin, is not an additional act which Christ performs in heaven, different from His death and resurrection. His intercession is the presence of His death and resurrection themselves before the Father' (Marvin P. Hoogland, 'Calvin's Perspective on the Exaltation of Christ in Comparison with the Post-Reformation Doctrine of the Two States', pp. 198f.). Cf. Wilhelm Niesel, *The Theology of Calvin*, pp. 153f.
52. Calvin's commentary on Heb. 7:25. For a discussion of this, see Staedtke, 'Königsherrschaft', pp. 205f.

It is fitting to draw some conclusions and to underline the soteriological import of Christ's threefold office of prophet, king, and priest. These three offices are not to be understood as 'historical stages of the work of redemption following one another ... but they form three aspects which are to be viewed as a whole'.[54] Christ's work of prophet concerns both his earthly and present heavenly ministries. He is king ever since his ascension, and yet his full kingdom awaits eschatological disclosure. His priestly work occurred at the cross and continues in intercession for his own.

The offices of Christ 'are not three compartments'. While maintaining the distinctions between the three, 'it is necessary to see their connection, each one always implies the two others.'[55] Christ's work of reconciliation, therefore, must be seen as the basis for his prophetic proclamation and the royal gifts of eternal life and protection he bestows on his church. Christ as prophet functions as inner teacher to actualize the priestly work of reconciliation and thereby usher sinners into the kingdom of God. Christ the king protects those who were purchased by Christ the priest and called by Christ the prophet. It is in terms of kingship that the eschatological consummation of the other two offices will occur. Those whom Christ reconciled to God and for whom he presently intercedes will experience consummate peace with God in his very presence. Those whom Christ as inner teacher has enlightened to receive the gospel will enjoy the eternal fruits of that Good News in the eschatological kingdom of God.

The three offices are both earthly and heavenly.[56] Jesus was prophet in his earthly ministry and continues as heavenly prophet,

53. *Institutes* II. xv. 6.

54. Uwe Gerber, *Christologische Entwürfe: Ein Arbeitsbuch*, p. 9.

55. Karl Barth, *La Confession de foi de l'église*, p. 35. Peter Toon agrees. 'The Significance of the Ascension for Believers,' *Bibliotheca Sacra* (January-March 1984: 20).

56. Willems and Weier, p. 29. Berkouwer summarises the unity of Christ's threefold office and its soteriological function (*Work of Christ*, p. 62): 'The office-bearing is not something rigid but has a wondrous

who teaches his people through his ministers by the Holy Spirit. Although Christ is chiefly king from ascension to *eschaton*, he announced his kingdom on earth and was declared to be king by his resurrection. Jesus was priest in his cross work of reconciliation and continues as priest in his heavenly work of intercession.

In *Institutes* II. xv, Calvin speaks of the Mediator's work of salvation by using the *munus triplex*. Not enough attention has been given to the transitional nature of that chapter of the *Institutes*. *Institutes* II. xii-xiv deals with the person of Christ, and II. xvi-xvii deals with his work. In chapter xv, Calvin via Christ's threefold office of prophet, king, and priest forms a bridge between preceding and subsequent chapters of *Institutes* II.[57] *Institutes* II. xv was one of Calvin's ways of telling his readers not to separate the person and work of Christ. To speak of Christ's person apart from his work is to fall into the perverse speculation of Osiander. To conceive of his work apart from his person would be meaningless – it is *his* work. The concept of office draws attention to the one who bears the office: the final prophet, the king of kings, the great high priest. At the same time Christ's offices are soteriological. 'The Calvinist theology does not develop an abstract doctrine of Christ's offices, but wants to make its soteriological *scopus* serviceable.'[58]

---

and saving effect. The name Christ, his official name, is inseparably connected with his name Jesus or Savior (*Institutes* II. xvi). For this reason we do not speak of three separate offices but of one indivisible office, even though, according to Calvin, this consists of three parts. In fulfilling this office he accomplishes the one work of salvation.' Cf. Willis, p. 85, Willems and Weier, p. 28, and Blaser, p. 45.

57. Although this has been noted by Blaser (p. 40), its full significance for Calvin's doctrine of the atonement has not been explored.

58. Staedtke, 'Königsherrschaft', p. 206. Blaser notes the importance of Christ's threefold office for believers. Christ the prophet brings the gospel, which gives His people freedom from the law's threats of judgment. Christ the king protects them and demands their obedience. Christ the priest procures eternal life for Christians by His death on the cross. Christ maintains that salvation by His continual heavenly intercession on their behalf (Blaser, p. 44).

4

CHRIST THE OBEDIENT SECOND ADAM

'Our Lord came forth as true man and took the person and name of Adam in order to take Adam's place in obeying the Father, to present our flesh as the price of satisfaction to God's righteous judgment, and in the same flesh, to pay the penalty that we had deserved' (*Inst.* II.xii.3).

In addition to the threefold office of Christ, Calvin uses six biblical themes of the atonement to describe the saving work of the Mediator. One of those themes portrays Christ as the obedient second Adam. There is a fundamental similarity between the first Adam and the second. In his exegesis of 1 Corinthians 15:45 Calvin writes: 'Adam and Christ are therefore, as it were, the two origins, or roots of the human race. That is why there is every justification for calling Adam the first man, and Christ the last.'[1] A solidarity is presupposed here between Adam and his descendants and between Christ and his. Both the first Adam and the second are identified with a people; they are the two 'roots' of the human race. As such their actions exert a tremendous effect upon the race. Adam fell into sin and thus brought all men and women under God's curse. Death, both spiritual and physical, was the tragic result. Christ through his actions brought righteousness, grace, and life to his people. Calvin's commentary on 1 Corinthians 15:21f. summarizes the respective effects of Adam and Christ upon the human race:

> Therefore, just as Adam did not die for himself alone, but for us all, so it follows that Christ, who is the antitype, did not rise again merely for Himself. For He came to restore everything which had been brought to ruin in Adam .... The cause of death is Adam, and we die

1. Calvin's commentary on 1 Cor. 15:45.

> in him; therefore Christ, whose function it is to restore what we have lost in Adam, is the cause of life for us.[2]

The notion of Christ as second Adam underscores his genuine humanity. Calvin explains that Christ partook of 'the human condition' in order to rescue Adam's descendants: 'I should also like to know why Paul calls Christ the "Second Adam" unless the human condition was ordained for him in order that he might lift Adam's descendants out of ruin.'[3] Calvin continues, 'Our Lord came forth as true man and took the person and the name of Adam in order to take Adam's place ....'[4] Both have true humanity. Hence, their names: the first Adam, and the second and last Adam.

How does Christ as the last Adam counter the destructive work of the first Adam? Calvin answers that 'He remedied the disobedience of Adam by a contrary act of obedience.'[5] In *Institutes* II. xii. 3 Calvin correlates Christ's obedience to his saving work:

> The second requirement of our reconciliation with God was this: that man, who by his disobedience had become lost, should by way of remedy counter it with obedience, satisfy God's judgment, and pay the penalties for sin. Accordingly, our Lord came forth as true man and took the person and name of Adam in order to take Adam's place in obeying the Father, to present our flesh as the price of satisfaction to God's righteous judgment, and in the same flesh, to pay the penalty that we had deserved.[6]

---

2. Hans Scholl perceptively notes that to Adam's fall (*Institutes* II. i-v) corresponds Christ's work (*Institutes* II. vi) (*Calvinus Catholicus*, p. 129).
3. *Institutes* II. xii. 7.
4. Ibid., II. xii. 3.
5. Calvin's commentary on Heb. 5:9.
6. Hans Scholl advances the thesis that Calvin reflects Irenaeus' doctrine of recapitulation at this point. He views *Institutes* II. vi as stamped with Irenaeus' thought. In spite of Scholl's work, I cannot accept his thesis for substantial and direct influence of Irenaeus upon Calvin's soteriology. Missing from Calvin's presentation of Christ's work are the very ideas which constituted recapitulation for Irenaeus: summation and iteration.

Calvin often spoke of Christ's work as the obedient second Adam in terms of restoration. The fall brought about conditions in which a restoration was needed. In the *Institutes* Calvin declares, 'But Paul, calling Christ the "Second Adam", sets the Fall, from which arose the necessity of restoring nature to its former condition, between man's first origin and the restoration which we obtain through Christ.'[7] The fall is mankind's 'catastrophic downfall'[8] by which everything was 'brought to ruin in Adam'.[9] Humanity's present plight is more tragic in the light of its original condition. Commenting on Hebrews 1:2, Calvin remarks:

> In the beginning God had established man as His son to be the heir of all good things; but the first man by his sin alienated from God both himself and his posterity and deprived them both of the blessing of God and of all good things.

Christ takes the name 'heir' because 'being made man and putting on the same nature as us, He took on Himself this heirship in order to restore to us what we had lost in Adam'. Christ is the 'Heir of all things' who enables believers to 'begin to enjoy the good things of God', which had been forfeited by Adam's sin.[10]

Christ sums up the human race in Himself by experiencing everything from infancy to old age. Christ also iterates Adam by retracing the first man's path point-by-point obediently and victoriously. Missing too are Irenaeus's favorite proof texts of Eph. 1:10 and Gal. 4:4 (for a summary of Irenaeus's doctrine of recapitulation, see J. N. D. Kelly, *Early Christian Doctrines*, 2nd ed. [New York: Har-Row, 1958], pp. 170-74). The reference to Irenaeus in *Institutes* II. vi. 4 is merely illustrative. The similarities between Irenaeus and Calvin are better explained by the fact that both were seeking to understand Christ's work in terms of Rom. 5:12-21. I therefore opt for a common biblical base as a better explanation for the similarities between Irenaeus and Calvin in soteriology than direct dependence of the latter upon the former. For Scholl's thesis, see Scholl, p.122.

7. *Institutes* II. xii. 7.
8. Calvin's commentary on 1 Cor. 15:45.
9. Calvin's commentary on 1 Cor. 15:21f.
10. Calvin's commentary on Heb. 1:2.

Therein is the restoration Christians enjoy: through Christ 'we recover what we had been deprived of'.[11] More specifically, our restoration consists of a 'better state',[12] even 'the life of heaven'.[13] Calvin's comments on the *textus classicus* for Christ's redemptive obedience, Romans 5:12-21, sum up well the Savior's role as second and last Adam:

> The meaning of the whole passage is that since Christ surpasses Adam, the sin of Adam is overcome by the righteousness of Christ. The curse of Adam is overturned by the grace of Christ, and the life which Christ bestows swallows up the death which came from Adam.[14]

There are two key aspects of Christ's obedience. Calvin views the entire earthly life of Jesus Christ as redemptive because in all things Christ obeyed the Father. The *Institutes* document this:

> How has Christ abolished sin, banished the separation between us and God, and acquired righteousness to render God favorable and kindly toward us? To this we can in general reply that he has achieved this for us by the whole course of his obedience .... In short, from the time when he took on the form of a servant, he began to pay the price of liberation in order to redeem us.[15]

Calvin's commentaries likewise agree that Christ's obedience extends to his whole life on earth.[16]

Christ's life of obedience culminated in 'His obedience unto death, even the death of the cross' (Phil. 2:8). In his comments on this Scripture Calvin says, 'He nevertheless became obedient to

---

11. Calvin's commentary on 1 Cor. 15:27.
12. Calvin's commentary on 1 Cor. 15:45.
13. Calvin's commentary on 1 Cor. 15:47. Cf. Calvin's commentary on 1 Cor. 15:21f.
14. Calvin's commentary on Rom. 5:17.
15. *Institutes* II. xvi. 5.
16. Calvin's commentaries on Matt. 26:17, John 2:13, and Gal. 4:4. Cf. T. H. L. Parker, *Calvin's Doctrine of the Knowledge of God*, pp. 85f.

His Father, even so far as to undergo death.'[17] Concerning Hebrews 10:10, Calvin teaches:

> Because it was Christ's example of obedience preeminently above all others to give Himself to die on the Cross, and because for this particular purpose He took on Himself the form of a servant, the apostle says that by offering Himself Christ fulfilled the command of the Father, and thus we have been sanctified.[18]

Calvin does not use the later Reformed terminology of the 'active' and 'passive' obedience of Christ. Yet he articulates the substance of that later Reformed distinction without using the very words.[19]

Calvin stresses the voluntary nature of Christ's obedience. The deity of Christ plays a fascinating part in this. Of the transfiguration, in which Christ's divine glory shone forth, Calvin writes:

> I have no doubt that Christ wanted to testify that He was not dragged unwillingly to death but went to it of His own free will, to offer the sacrifice of obedience to His Father .... For it is always clear that it would have been no more difficult for Christ to give His body immunity from death than to adorn it with heavenly glory. And so we learn that He was subject to death because He wished to be, that He was crucified because He offered Himself.[20]

---

17. Calvin's commentary on Phil. 2:8. Conditt was correct in writing: 'though He rendered obedience all of His life, it was chiefly in His death at the hands of men that Christ effected man's reconciliation' (Marion W. Conditt, 'More Acceptable Than Sacrifice: Ethics and Election as Obedience to God's Will in the Theology of Calvin' [Th.D. dissertation, University of Basel, 1973], p. 41).
18. Cf. Calvin's commentary on Matt. 26:24 and T. H. L. Parker, *The Oracles of God: An Introduction to the Preaching of John Calvin* (London: Lutterworth, 1947), pp. 87f.
19. Berkouwer concurs with this conclusion, and puts the matter in proper perspective: 'Calvin indeed strongly emphasized ... the unity of Christ's obedience as wholly oriented to the reconciliation, but even with him the twofold aspect is clearly evident when he views Christ's whole life as obedience' (G. C. Berkouwer, *The Work of Christ*, p.321).
20. Calvin's commentary on Matt. 17:1.

The Gospel of John records that when the soldiers came to arrest Jesus Christ, his spoken reply knocked them to the ground. Why should he do that when he was about to surrender to his foes? Calvin answers in his commentary on John 18:12: 'It serves to remove the stumblingblock of our thinking that Christ yielded as if overcome through weakness, and secondly, it proves that He suffered death completely voluntarily.'[21]

If Christ's deity serves to emphasize the voluntary nature of his obedience, his humanity underlines the reality of that submission to the Father's will. The Son of God was not play-acting in the garden. Rather, the agony of Gethsemane was real. As Calvin makes clear in his commentary on John 12:27:

> Although He may legitimately dread death, yet when He considers why He was sent and what His office of Mediator demands, He offers to His Father the dread conceived of His natural senses, that it might be subdued – or rather, having subdued it, He prepares freely and willingly to execute God's command.[22]

Calvin's commentary on Isaiah 53:11 demonstrates the nexus between Christ's humanity, His voluntary obedience, and our redemption:

> He shows that Christ justifies us, not only as he is God, but also as he is man; for in our flesh he procured righteousness for us. He does not say, 'the Son', but 'My servant', that we may not only view him as God, but may contemplate his human nature, in which he performed that obedience by which we are acquitted before God.[23]

In *Institutes* II. xvi. 5, Calvin spells out that Christ's voluntary obedience as the second Adam was essential for our salvation:

---

21. Cf. Calvin's commentary on Matt. 26:18 for a similar testimony to the connection between Christ's deity and His voluntary obedience.
22. Cf. Calvin's commentaries on John 18:1 and Matt. 26:36.
23. E. D. Willis aptly summarizes the indispensability of Christ's humanity for His voluntary obedience, which wrought our salvation: 'The full humanity is absolutely indispensable because it constitutes the instrument

> Yet to define the way of salvation more exactly, Scripture ascribes this as peculiar and proper to Christ's death.... And truly, even in death itself his willing obedience is the important thing because a sacrifice not offered voluntarily would not have furthered righteousness.[24]

In various places in his commentaries Calvin specifically notes the necessity of Christ's voluntary obedience for the salvation of his people:

> He had to submit to death of His own free will to destroy the wilful disobedience of men by His own obedience.

---

of Christ's redemptive obedience. What is saving in Christ's teaching, miracles, and death is not simply that they occurred, but that they occurred voluntarily. The heart of the reconstituting act is the free obedience of the Second Adam which displaces the wilful disobedience of the first Adam' (E. David Willis, *Calvin's Catholic Christology*, pp. 84f.). Van Buren takes Calvin to task here for failing to give Christ's deity enough place in the work of redemption: 'We cannot speak of the obedience of Christ in Calvin's theology without speaking of the strong emphasis he puts on the idea that this obedience was performed in Christ's human nature only.... The question remains as to the complete involvement of God in the substitutionary work of Christ' (Paul Van Buren, *Christ in Our Place*, pp. 38f.). Van Buren's remarks are most unfortunate in the light of Calvin's contest with F. Stancaro, in which Calvin is pressed to make more emphatic statements on Christ procuring salvation in both natures. In his second letter to Stancaro, Calvin writes: 'Similarly, it was the function of the mediator to acquire righteousness for us by His obedience and so become the servant of the Father; it would be erroneous to ascribe this to the divine nature; nevertheless, the very acquisition of righteousness does borrow its force from the divine nature' (Joseph N. Tylenda, 'The Controversy on Christ the Mediator', p. 150). In view of this evidence Wendel's conclusion must be accepted: 'Although, properly speaking, there can be no question of any obedience by Christ, except according to his human nature, it was the whole of Jesus Christ, in his capacity of mediator, who submitted himself to the Father and who, by his obedience, obtained for us the divine reconciliation' (François Wendel, *Calvin: Origins and Development of His Religious Thought*, p. 226).

24. Calvin's commentaries on Matt. 17:24; 26:1, and John 19:12.

> Here the Prophet applauds the obedience of Christ in suffering death; for if his death had not been voluntary, he would not have been regarded as having satisfied for our disobedience.[25]

Such was Calvin's first theme of reconciliation. Christ is the second Adam, who by his voluntary obedience in life and especially in death countered the disobedience of our first father, Adam, and restored eternal life and all good things to his people.[26]

The words of Randall C. Zachman form a fitting conclusion to this chapter: 'The Son of God becomes the Son of Adam, and therefore the second Adam, in order to manifest God in the creaturely sphere by being the fountain of every good set forth by God the Father for sinful creatures, to restore to sinful humanity every good thing that it lost in Adam and to free sinful humanity from every evil thing that it acquired in Adam.'[27]

---

25. Calvin's commentaries on Acts 8:32 and Isa. 53:7. Cf. Calvin's commentary on John 14:30. Conditt accurately sums up the matter when he writes of Christ, 'Until He surrendered Himself willingly His death could not atone for the purposeful rebellion of Adam' (Conditt, p. 42).
26. Brian Armstrong's study of 'The Concept of Restoration/Restitution in Calvin' augments this chapter. One sample: 'Calvin's use of "restoration" terminology clearly underlines his emphasis on the idea that God, in his redemptive activity, is not creating a new order, but rather providing the way by which his original creation is being restored.' *Calvinus Servus Christi*, ed. Wilhelm Heinrich Neuser (Budapest: Presseabteilung des Raday-Kollegiums, 1988), p. 147.
27. Randall C. Zachman, 'Jesus Christ as the Image of God in Calvin's Theology,' *Calvin Theological Journal* 25 (1990): 49.

5

CHRIST THE VICTOR

'Therefore, by his wrestling hand to hand with the devil's power, with the dread of death, with the pains of hell, he was victorious and triumphed over them, that in death we may now not fear those things which our Prince has swallowed up' (*Inst.* II. xvi.11).

One of Calvin's favorite themes of the atonement is Christ as victor, who conquers the foes of his people. This is the 'classical theme' popularized by Gustaf Aulén in his book, *Christus Victor*.[1] Powerful enemies are set against the human race. The devil, death, sin and the world are tenacious foes out to destroy humankind.

In his commentary on 2 Corinthians Calvin tells how the devil's main objective is to keep sinners from believing the gospel.

---

1. Gustaf Aulén, *Christus Victor: An Historical Study of the Three Main Types of the Idea of the Atonement*, trans. A. G. Hebert (New York: Macmillan, 1969). Aulén's work is open to criticism. He oversimplified the biblical materials on the atonement and found them teaching only one thing – the *Christus Victor* theme. He did the same for individuals (Irenaeus and Luther) as well as for whole periods of theological activity (e.g., the patristic period). Still, credit is due Aulén for recovering an atonement motif that has an important place in the Bible, the patristic writers, and the works of the major Reformers. It is unfortunate, as Hall points out, that in *Christus Victor*, 'Gustav Aulén ignored Calvin's doctrine of the atonement.' This should not surprise us, however, for 'there is also relatively little recognition of the Christus Victor element in Calvin's thought among Calvin scholars' (Charles A. M. Hall, *With the Spirit's Sword*, p. 90). To call the victory theme 'Calvin's most recurrent theme', as Jansen does, is to overstate the case (John F. Jansen, *Calvin's Doctrine of the Work of Christ*, p. 88). Nevertheless, the concept of Christ's saving work as a mighty victory occupies a large place in Calvin's thought and deserves a corresponding place in any consideration of his doctrine of the atonement.

Attacking the mental processes, 'the devil has blinded their understanding' to keep the unsaved from trusting Christ as Savior.[2]

Death, another powerful foe, wields its favorite weapon, fear. Calvin writes of the 'misery of the life of those who are afraid of death'. They are most pitiable creatures whose very life is a 'state of servitude' and one of 'constant anxiety' because of their fear of dying. Death 'must of necessity be terrible to those who think of it without Christ'.[3]

Sin is a third adversary who preys upon the human race. It is a cruel master: 'outside of Christ ... sin ... reigns in us', as Calvin says in his Ephesians commentary.[4]

The world, understood as that sinful world system that is opposed to Christ's kingdom, is a fourth opponent. While commenting on 1 John, Calvin explains that the world is filled 'with corruptions of every kind and the abyss of all evils ... by which man is captivated to withdraw from God'.[5]

It is into this desperate situation that Christ the champion comes. Men and women who are powerless against such mighty foes should be thankful that Christ overcomes their enemies for them. Sometimes Calvin links the adversaries, as in his commentary on Isaiah 53:12: 'Thus also Christ as a valiant and illustrious general, triumphed over the enemies whom he had vanquished .... For us Christ subdued death, the world, and the devil.'[6] Elsewhere Calvin lists the enemies singly and rejoices in the victory through Christ. In Christ's death is his people's 'secure triumphing over death, since the Son of God has endured it in our place, and struggling with it has emerged the victor.'[7] Celebrating the victory of Christians over Satan through Christ, Calvin asks rhetorically, 'For to what purpose was Christ sanctified by the Father, if not to free men from the devil's tyranny and overthrow his kingdom?'[8]

---

2. Calvin's commentary on 2 Cor. 4:4.
3. Calvin's commentary on Heb. 2:15.
4. Calvin's commentary on Eph. 2:1.
5. Calvin's commentary on 1 John 2:15.
6. Cf. Calvin's commentaries on John 13:31 and Eph. 4:8.
7. Calvin's commentary on John 19:30.

Sounding very much like Luther, Calvin recounts Christ's conquest of sin and vitiation of the curse of the law in his commentary on 1 Corinthians 15:57: 'But Christ has conquered sin, and by His conquest has obtained the victory for us, and redeemed us from the curse of the Law .... We have every right then, to taunt death as a conquered power, because Christ's victory is our victory.'[9] These are the enemies over which Christ has triumphed on behalf of his people. To better appreciate Calvin's victory theme of the atonement, it is important to take a closer look at the victor himself.

The picture of Christ the victor lays great weight on his deity:

> For the same reason it was also imperative that he who was to become our Redeemer be true God and true man. It was his task to swallow up death. Who but the Life could do this? It was his task to conquer sin. Who but very Righteousness could do this? It was his task to rout out the powers of world and air. Who but a power higher than world and air could do this? Now where does life or righteousness or lordship and authority of heaven lie but with God alone? Therefore our most merciful God, when he willed that we be redeemed, made himself our Redeemer in the person of his only-begotten Son.[10]

Their adversaries are too strong for God's people to overcome. Hence if they are to be delivered, it is God himself who must undertake their cause for them. Calvin's exegesis of the messianic title 'Mighty God' in Isaiah 9:6 demonstrates the indispensability of Christ the champion's deity for the victory of believers:

> With good reason does he call him strong or mighty, because our contest is with the devil, death and sin (Eph. 6:12), enemies too powerful and strong, by whom we would be immediately vanquished, if the strength of Christ had not rendered us invincible. Thus we learn from this title that there is in Christ abundance of protection for defending our salvation, so that we desire nothing beyond him; for he is God, who is pleased to show himself strong on our behalf.[11]

---

8. Calvin's commentary on Mark 1:21.
9. Cf. *Luther's Works* 26:158-60.
10. *Institutes* II. xii. 2. 11. Calvin's commentary on Isa. 9:6.

The champion, Jesus Christ, must be God to defeat believers' foes. He must be man, too, if the victory is to benefit his people and become their victory. The humanity of Christ plays an important dual role in Calvin's image of Christ as victor. First, it underscores the reality of the battle. In his comments on Christ's struggle in the garden of Gethsemane, Calvin writes of the words, 'Arise, let us be going':

> These words reveal that since His prayer, He had found new reserves of arms. Before He had been willing enough for death, but at the sudden crisis He had a serious struggle with the weakness of the flesh, till He might have been glad to withdraw from death, if the good consent of the Father had been allowed Him. With prayers and tears He gained new strength from heaven: not that any lack of strength had ever made Him waver, but in the weakness of the flesh, which He had freely assumed, He wished to wrestle in anguish, in painful and hard combat, that in His own person He might win the victory for us.[12]

It is important to note here that Christ's struggles were not merely physical. The physical burdens were terrible; but the spiritual aspects of his suffering were the greater cause of the Savior's fear and dread. Calvin makes that clear:

> We must look to the point of His fear. Why did He dread death except that He saw in it the curse of God, and that He had to wrestle with the sum total of human guilt, and with the very powers of darkness themselves. Hence the fear and anxiety, because the judgment of God is more than terrifying. He got what He wanted inasmuch as He emerged from the pains of death as Conqueror, was upheld by the saving hand of the Father, and after a brief encounter gained a glorious victory over Satan, sin, and the powers of hell.[13]

Christ's humanity highlights the reality of his contest with the enemies. Secondly, it serves to accent the substitutionary nature of his victory. Contending for the true humanity of Christ, Calvin

---

12. Calvin's commentary on Matt. 26:46.
13. Calvin's commentary on Heb. 5:7.

reports that he regards the first mention of redemption in Scripture, Genesis 3:15, as a statement of the *Christus Victor* theme. Christ's victory was a victory for the human race because he was a real man:

> If we carefully weigh Moses' testimony – where he says that the seed of the woman will crush the serpent's head – the controversy will be completely resolved. For the statement there concerns not only Christ but the whole of mankind. Since we must acquire victory through Christ, God declares in general terms that the woman's offspring is to prevail over the devil. Hence it follows that Christ was begotten of mankind, for in addressing Eve it was God's intention to raise her hope that she should not be overwhelmed with despair.[14]

Calvin states the matter succinctly in the *Institutes*: 'Clothed with our flesh he vanquished death and sin together that the victory and triumph might be ours.'[15] The commentaries of Calvin likewise attest to the fact that Christ's humanity assures believers that his victory is theirs.[16]

Calvin's conception of the saving work of Christ is a broad one. Although he sees the cross as the heart of the atonement, he does not confine the work of Christ to the cross. The incarnation, the life of Christ, the crucifixion, the descent, the resurrection, the ascension, and the second coming of Christ are all redemptive. They are components of one grand redemptive plan, the center of

---

14. *Institutes* II. xiii. 2.
15. Ibid., II. xii. 3.
16. Cf. Calvin's commentaries on Matt. 27:50, Acts 2:24, and 8:32. It was previously mentioned that Aulén omitted Calvin's doctrine of the work of Christ from *Christus Victor*. This omission is unfortunate because Calvin's emphasis on Christ as conqueror in both divine and human natures could have served as a corrective to Aulén's stress on Christ's deity to the neglect of his humanity. Leon Morris was correct when he criticized Aulén: 'Over and over he insists that the atonement is from first to last God's work. He concentrates on the theme that God in Christ has won the victory over the forces of evil. The manhood of our Lord had no real part to play in the work of the atonement' (Leon Morris, *The Cross in the New Testament* [Grand Rapids: Eerdmans, 1965], pp. 373f.).

which is the cross. The breadth of Calvin's doctrine of the atonement is easily seen in terms of the victory theme. In his commentary on Hebrews 2:14, Calvin tells how the incarnation was redemptive:

> The Son of God ... was made man to share the same state and nature as us.... He put on our nature in order to submit Himself to the state of death.... He has freed us from a diabolical tyranny.... The devil himself has been laid low as to be of no more account, as if he did not exist.[17]

Christ's earthly life was a contest with Satan and the forces of evil, over which he repeatedly emerged victorious. As Calvin explains in his exposition of Matthew 4:1, Satan attacked Christ in the temptation because he knew that Christ 'was being trained for man's redemption'. Thus 'it was our salvation that he then attacked in the Person of Christ'. And yet because of his love for his own, 'The Son of God willingly underwent the temptations ... and met the devil in a set trial of strength, that by His victory He might win us the triumph.'[18]

In the expulsion of demons Christ demonstrated his authority over the kingdom of Satan. In his commentaries on the Gospels Calvin teaches:

> Further, they [the demons] are brought to a halt in mid-career by Christ's secret force, that by their expulsion He may reveal Himself as men's Deliverer.
>
> So by setting men's physical faculties free from the tyranny of the devil, He testified that He was sent by His Father to be the champion who would destroy his spiritual tyranny over their souls.[19]

---

17. Cf. Calvin's commentary on 1 John 3:8. In his book on spiritual warfare in Calvin's theology, Charles Hall tells how the incarnation of the Son of God is redemptive: 'The Mighty One invades the kingdom of Satan by firmly establishing himself on and within the struggle's decisive battleground: man.... The *Christus Victor* motif in soteriology corresponds to a Christology of the Divine Invader' (Hall, pp. 83f.).
18. Calvin's commentary on Matt. 4:1.

Christ's miracles, especially the exorcisms, were a series of minor conflicts, which led up to the great battle of the cross. It was there, in death itself, that the fiercest fight was fought and won by the Lord Jesus Christ. Calvin describes the plight of sinners and Christ's hard-won triumph over their deadly foes:

> Death held us captive under its yoke; Christ, in our stead, gave himself over to its power to deliver us from it.... He differed from us, however, in this respect: he let himself be swallowed up by death, as it were, not to be engulfed in its abyss, but rather to engulf it that must soon have engulfed us; he let himself be subjected to it, not to be overwhelmed by its power, but rather to lay it low, when it was threatening us and exulting over our fallen state. Finally, his purpose was 'that through death he might destroy him who had the power of death, that is, the devil....'[20]

One can appreciate the victory at the cross only after realizing the shame attached to it. To the Hebrews the cross was accursed; to the Romans the cross was an instrument of condemnation. Christ the mighty victor transformed the hated cross into 'a triumphal chariot', as Calvin informs his readers in the *Institutes*:

> Yet we must not understand that he fell under a curse that overwhelmed him; rather – in taking the curse upon himself – he crushed, broke, and scattered its whole force. Hence faith apprehends an acquittal in the condemnation of Christ, a blessing in his curse. Paul with good reason, therefore, magnificently proclaims the triumph that Christ obtained for himself on the cross, as if the cross, which was full of shame, had been changed into a triumphal chariot![21]

In his commentaries Calvin employs the figure of the cross of Christ as 'a splendid chariot' in which 'He made triumph over His enemies and ours' to proclaim Christ's death as a great victory.[22]

---

19. Calvin's commentaries on Mark 5:6 and Matt. 12:29.
20. *Institutes* II. xvi. 7.
21. Ibid., II. xvi. 6.
22. Calvin's commentary on Luke 23:16. Cf. Calvin's commentaries on John 12:32 and Col. 2:15. Hall captures the centrality of the cross in

Calvin does not understand the descent into hell in the medieval manner of a literal descent of Christ into the nether world. Rather, the descent for Calvin is Christ's spiritual agony on the cross. This too is depicted in terms of victory in the *Institutes*:

> The apostle, recalling this fruit of victory, asserts the same thing, that they were 'delivered who through the fear of death were subject to lifelong bondage.' He had, therefore, to conquer that fear which by nature continually torments and oppresses all mortals. This he could do only by fighting it.... Therefore, by his wrestling hand to hand with the devil's power, with the dread of death, with the pains of hell, he was victorious and triumphed over them, that in death we may now not fear those things which our Prince has swallowed up.[23]

It is in the resurrection of Christ that his victory and that of his people is supremely displayed. His triumph at the cross is known only because he arose from the grave. In the *Institutes*, Calvin puts the matter plainly:

Calvin's *Christus Victor* theme: 'In the connected series of victories which make up the earthly history of Jesus, the decisive event which is the sum of all previous conquests and the necessary precondition of those that follow is his suffering and death on the cross. What is accomplished in this decisive event? The central answer lies in the fact that there man's sin has been dealt with, atoned for, washed away, forgiven; and thus, to put the whole in terms of the spiritual warfare, the power of sin over men's lives has been broken' (Hall, p. 105).

23. *Institutes* II. xvi. 11. Mary Rakow tells how Calvin's interpretation of the descent affected the victory theme of the atonement: 'If the traditional treatment of the descent was one of victory already won and a journey of triumph to the underworld, Calvin's descent is one through which victory is achieved' (Mary Rakow, 'Christ's Descent into Hell: Calvin's Interpretation', *Religion in Life* 43 [1974]: 224). Rakow's article accurately depicts Calvin's interpretation of the descent in the light of medieval antecedents. Robert M. Brenton presents Calvin's view of the descent in light of his soteriology and makes present application in 'Calvin's Confession of Christ's Descent into Hell in the Context of the Doctrine of Redemption: An Historical and Hermeneutical Inquiry' (Th.M. thesis, Calvin Theological Seminary, 1993).

> For as he, in rising again, came forth victor over death, so the victory of our faith lies in his resurrection alone.... For how could he by dying have freed us from death if he himself succumbed to death? How could he have acquired victory for us if he had failed in the struggle? Therefore, we divide the substance of our salvation between Christ's death and resurrection as follows: through his death, sin was wiped out and death extinguished; through his resurrection, righteousness was restored and life raised up, so that – thanks to his resurrection – his death manifested its power and efficacy in us.[24]

Calvin's commentaries likewise convey the importance of Christ's resurrection for redemption. Commenting on 1 Corinthians 15 Calvin laments the situation of believers if Christ had not been raised from the dead:

> For what is there left if Christ has been devoured by death, if He has been annihilated, if He has been crushed by the curse of sin, if, finally, He has surrendered to Satan?... But in the mere death of Christ we can discover nothing but grounds for despair; for someone who has been completely conquered by death cannot effect the salvation of others.[25]

In his commentary on the resurrection narrative in Matthew, Calvin celebrates the victory won for Christians by their Savior:

> This is the source of our lively confidence in our reconciliation with God, that Christ came forth from hell as Victor over death, and showed that the power of the new life was in His hands.... Then was our adoption assured; Christ in resurrection exerted the power of His Spirit and proved Himself Son of God.[26]

Calvin also presents Christ's ascension and session (his being seated with the Father in heaven) in terms of victory:

---

24. *Institutes* II. xvi. 13.
25. Calvin's commentary on 1 Cor. 15:14.
26. Calvin's commentary on Matt. 28:1. Cf. Calvin's commentary on 1 Pet. 1:21. Hall underscores the importance of Christ's resurrection for Calvin's victory theme of the atonement: 'Substantially, Christ's

> Thirdly, faith comprehends his might, in which reposes our strength, power, wealth, and glorying against hell. 'When he ascended into heaven he led captivity captive' (Eph. 4:8), and despoiling his enemies, he enriched his own people, and daily lavishes spiritual riches upon them. He therefore sits on high ... that he may ... restrain the raging enemies of his cross and of our salvation by the strength of his hand, and finally hold all power in heaven and on earth. All this he does until he shall lay low all his enemies ... and complete the building of his church.[27]

The ascension and session are thus transitional between Christ's procuring victory in his death and resurrection and the final outward display of that triumph in the *eschaton*. In that day believers will as 'a willing people run to Christ ... to show themselves as obedient subjects.' Yet toward the ungodly 'Christ is immediately armed with power to destroy, in the day of his wrath, kings and armies who are hostile to him.'[28]

Calvin's second theme of the atonement portrays Christ as the divine-human victor who defeats sin, death, the world, and Satan chiefly through his death and resurrection and thereby gains a great victory for every believer.

---

resurrection is itself a conquest, in fact the resurrection may be thought of as *the* victory which includes in itself the triumph of Christ's passion and death' (Hall, p. 99). Cf. Arthur Dakin, *Calvinism* (London: Duckworth, 1941), p. 53.

27. *Institutes* II. xvi. 16. Cf. ibid., II. xvi. 14.

28. Calvin's commentary on Ps. 2:9. Karl Barth uses an illustration from chess of a player defeated and yet playing on until checkmated to depict Christ's victory over Satan as won and yet to be revealed fully in the future (Barth, *La Confession de foi de l'église*, p. 56).

6

CHRIST OUR LEGAL SUBSTITUTE

'As no one can succeed in his accusation when the judge absolves, so there remains no condemnation, when the laws have been satisfied and the penalty already paid. Christ is the One who once suffered the punishment due to us, and thereby professed that He took our place in order to deliver us. Anyone, therefore, who desires to condemn us after this must kill Christ Himself again' (Calvin's commentary on Romans 8:34).

Calvin also teaches a legal theme of the atonement in which Christ both fulfilled the law on behalf of his people during his life and took the condemnation sinners deserve in his death. It is difficult to determine which of the three atonement themes plays the greatest role in Calvin's thought: the *Christus Victor* theme (considered in the previous chapter), the sacrificial theme (the subject of the next chapter), or the legal theme (treated here). All three figure prominently in Calvin's doctrine of the work of Christ.

Before considering Christ's work in legal terms, it is helpful to summarize some of Calvin's ideas about the law. It is important to see the relation between law-giver and law in Calvin's thought. In *Institutes* II. vii, Calvin maintains that the law as the expression of God's character is 'a perfect pattern of righteousness'.[1] Later in that chapter he notes that the law contains the 'knowledge of the divine will'. Hence Calvin does not understand the law in an impersonal sense as an abstract code; it is 'the best instrument ... to learn more thoroughly each day the nature of the Lord's will'.[2] In *Institutes* II. viii. 5, he says that the law is 'the perfect rule of

---

1. *Institutes* II. vii. 13.
2. Ibid., II. vii. 12. Cf. Robert A. Gessert, 'The Integrity of Faith: An Inquiry into the Meaning of Law in the Thought of John Calvin,' *Scottish Journal of Theology* 13 (1960): 250f., and John H. Leith, 'Creation

righteousness' and that the Lord 'has referred all its parts to his will'.[3]

Calvin holds that conditional salvation is offered by the law: 'We cannot gainsay that the reward of eternal salvation awaits complete obedience to the law, as the Lord had promised.' He is quick to add, however, 'Because observance of the law is found in none of us, we are excluded from the promises of life, and fall back into the mere curse.'[4] We can never merit salvation by keeping the law because we are sinners. Thus the ten commandments, which accurately reveal God's will and the way to salvation, become for sinners an instrument of condemnation as the law exposes their sins. Calvin clearly expresses this in his commentary on Galatians:

> All who wish to be justified by the works of the law are declared to be liable to the curse. But how does he prove this? The sentence of the law is that all who have transgressed any part of the law are accursed. Let us see if there is any man living who satisfies the law. It is certain that none has been or ever can be found. Every individual is here condemned.[5]

In *Institutes* II. xvi. 1, Calvin communicates why sinners need another to keep the law in their place:

> No one can descend into himself and seriously consider who he is without feeling God's wrath and hostility toward him. Accordingly, he must anxiously seek ways and means to appease God – and this

---

and Redemption; Law and Gospel in the Theology of John Calvin', in *A Reexamination of Lutheran and Reformed Traditions* (New York: Published jointly by representatives of the North American Area of the World Alliance of Reformed Churches Holding the Presbyterian Order and the U.S.A. National Committee of the Lutheran World Federation, 1965), pp. 50f.

3. See Edward A. Dowey, *The Knowledge of God in Calvin's Theology*, pp. 222-42, for an excellent discussion of Calvin's concept of law.
4. *Institutes* II. vii. 3. Cf. Dowey, p. 227.
5. Calvin's commentary on Gal. 3:10.

> demands a satisfaction. No common assurance is required, for God's wrath and curse always lie upon sinners until they are absolved of guilt. Since he is a righteous Judge, he does not allow his law to be broken without punishment, but is equipped to avenge it.[6]

It is good to examine the positive side of Christ's fulfillment of the law first. In his commentaries on the Gospels Calvin repeatedly affirms that Christ kept every detail of the law as his people's legal substitute. He submitted to baptism at the hands of John the Baptist 'to offer his Father full obedience'. Commenting on Jesus' words 'for in this way it is fitting for us to fulfill all righteousness', Calvin writes: 'The word *righteousness* often has the same effect in Scripture as observance of the law, and so this passage may be expounded thus: It is necessary for Christ, from His free submission to the law, to keep it in every part.'[7] Inasmuch as Jesus Christ went up to Jerusalem to keep the Passover, Calvin remarks, 'Since the Son of God was subject to the law for our sake, He wished by observing precisely all the law's commands, to show Himself a type of complete submission and obedience.'[8] Calvin goes to great lengths to maintain his position that Jesus fulfilled the law down to the smallest detail. Calvin feels constrained to prove that Christ was correct in observing the Passover on Good Friday, rather than on Saturday when the Jewish nation as a whole celebrated it publicly.

> Now if it were a matter of custom to link the two days into one (as the Jews themselves admit and is found in their ancient records), it is quite reasonable to guess that Christ who celebrated the Passover

---

6. T. H. L. Parker sums up Christ's positive and negative fulfillment of the law: 'The law has been fulfilled on earth by a man – by the man in whom the Law-giver himself has entered into a union with all men; fulfilled positively in that he has obeyed it perfectly, negatively in that he has suffered the punishment for breaking the Law incurred by all men' (T. H. L. Parker, *John Calvin: A Biography* [Philadelphia: Westminster, 1975], p. 38).
7. Calvin's commentary on Matt. 3:15.
8. Calvin's commentary on John 2:13.

> on the eve of the sabbath kept to the day appointed by the Law. We know the particular care He gave not to depart one jot from the letter of the Law. Seeing He wished to be bound by the Law, that He might relieve us of its yoke, He forgot not the least article of its oversight.[9]

It was as his people's substitute that Jesus Christ fulfilled the law in such detail. Calvin teaches this at least twice in his commentaries on Paul's Epistles:

> Christ submitted Himself to the bondage of the Law, although He was not otherwise a debtor to its demands, in order that, in the words of the apostle, He might redeem those who were under the Law (Gal. 4:5).
>
> Christ the Son of God, who was by right exempt from all subjection, became subject to the law. Why? In our name, that He might obtain freedom for us.... In the same way Christ chose to become liable to keep the law that He might obtain exemption for us.[10]

The obedience of Christ to the law is the basis of justification. God declares sinners righteous on the basis of Christ's righteousness. In his exegesis of Romans 5:19 Calvin declares:

> When he afterwards states that we are made righteous by the obedience of Christ, we deduce from this that Christ, in satisfying the Father, has procured righteousness for us. It follows from this that righteousness exists in Christ as a property, but that that which belongs properly to Christ is imputed to us. At the same time he explains the character of the righteousness of Christ by referring to it as *obedience*.[11]

Christ was his people's legal substitute not only in fulfilling

---

9. Calvin's commentary on Matt. 26:17.
10. Calvin's commentaries on Rom. 6:14 and Gal. 4:4. Cf. Van Buren's statement of Christ's substitutionary fulfillment of the law on behalf of sinners (Paul Van Buren, *Christ in Our Place*, p. 31).
11. Calvin's commentary on Rom. 5:19. For a discussion of Christ's fulfillment of the law as the ground of believers' justification, see Tjarko Stadtland, *Rechtfertigung und Heiligung bei Calvin*, p. 134.

the law perfectly throughout his life, but also by taking their condemnation on the cross of Calvary. In *Institutes* II. xvi, Calvin offers a theological exposition of the Apostles' Creed. The fact that Christ was condemned by Pontius Pilate has great importance for Calvin. Pilate, although a wicked man, was nevertheless God's instrument. Calvin explains:

> The curse caused by our guilt was awaiting us at God's heavenly judgment seat. Accordingly, Scripture first relates Christ's condemnation before Pontius Pilate, governor of Judea, to teach us that the penalty to which we were subject had been imposed upon this righteous man. We could not escape God's dreadful judgment. To deliver us from it, Christ allowed himself to be condemned before a mortal man – even a wicked and profane man.[12]

In his comments on Luke 22:37 Calvin expresses the same idea by labelling Christ 'a criminal':

> Christ means that the whole range of His task is not complete until He has been reckoned with the evil-doers and criminals, as one of that order.... Christ who could not have been their Redeemer in any other sense than by taking on Himself the shame and disgrace of a criminal.... Isaiah plainly testified that to clear us of the guilt of our crimes the penalty must be transferred to Him.... Christ was put under the condemnation which we had all merited, and reckoned among the godless....[13]

It is of utmost importance to note that Pilate's verdict of condemnation was not the only sentence pronounced that day. There was another verdict, which preceded the sentence of condemnation:

> For it is very important for us to know that Pilate did not condemn Christ before he himself had acquitted Him three or four times, so that we may learn from it that it was not on His own account that He was condemned but for our sin.[14]

---

12. *Institutes* II. xvi. 5.
13. Calvin's commentary on Luke 22:37.
14. Calvin's commentary on John 19:12.

Christ's acquittal proclaims his innocence and underlines the substitutionary nature of his condemnation. He was not condemned for his own sins (he had none), but for the sins of others, as Calvin asserts in his exposition of Matthew 27:19:

> We should rather hold that Christ's innocence was given many proofs by God the Father to make it clear that for another's (that is, our own) sake He met His death. He wished Pilate often to speak of His acquittal before condemning Him, so that in His undeserved condemnation the satisfaction won for our sins should blaze out.[15]

Great benefits accrue to every believer because of that double verdict rendered by an evil, earthly judge. The declarations of innocence and condemnation pronounced upon the Son of God result in the removal of guilt and the opening of free access to God's heavenly throne, as Calvin told in his commentary on Matthew 27:11:

> The Son of God wished to stand bound before an earthly judge and there submit to the death sentence, that we might not doubt that we are freed of guilt and free to approach to the heavenly throne of God. If we consider what benefits we have in Christ's standing trial before Pilate, the stain of such base submission will immediately be removed.... God's Son stood trial before a mortal man and suffered accusation and condemnation, that we might stand without fear in the presence of God.[16]

Calvin uses many images to express Christ's taking the condemnation of believers when he died for their sins. The ideas of penalty and punishment come easily to Calvin's mind when he speaks of Christ our legal substitute. Concerning Isaiah 53:6, 'And the LORD hath laid on him the iniquity of us all' (KJV), Calvin pens these words:

> Our sins are a heavy load; but they are laid on Christ, by whom we are freed from the load. Thus, when we were ruined, and, being

15. Cf. Calvin's commentary on Matt. 27:24.
16. Cf. Calvin's commentary on Matt. 27:26.

> estranged from God, were hastening to hell, Christ took upon him the filthiness of our iniquities, in order to rescue us from everlasting destruction. This must refer exclusively to guilt and punishment; for he was free from sin.[17]

Because Christ took their penalty and suffered punishment for their sins, believers need fear no judgment:

> As no one can succeed in his accusation when the judge absolves, so there remains no condemnation, when the laws have been satisfied and the penalty already paid. Christ is the One who once suffered the punishment due to us, and thereby professed that He took our place in order to deliver us. Anyone, therefore, who desires to condemn us after this must kill Christ Himself again. But Christ has not only died, He has also come forth as conqueror of death, and triumphed over its power by His resurrection.[18]

Sounding much like Luther, Calvin in the *Institutes* tells of Christ 'the sinner' who was burdened with the sins of his people:

> ... surely that he might die in the place of the sinner, not of the righteous or innocent man. For he suffered death not because of innocence but because of sin.... Thus we shall behold the person of a sinner and evil-doer represented in Christ, yet from his shining innocence it will at the same time be obvious that he was burdened with another's sin rather than his own.[19]

The thought of substitution is prominent when Calvin describes Christ 'the sinner' in his commentary on 2 Corinthians 5:21:

> How can we become righteous before God? In the same way as Christ became a sinner. For He took, as it were, our person, that He might be the offender in our name and thus might be reckoned a sinner, not because of his own offences but because of those of

---

17. Calvin's commentary on Isa. 53:6.
18. Calvin's commentary on Rom. 8:34. Cf. Calvin's commentaries on Rom. 4:25 and Gal. 2:19.
19. *Institutes* II. xvi. 5. Cf. Luther's *Works* 26:277-78.

> others, since He himself was pure and free from every fault and bore the penalty that was our due and not His own.[20]

It is significant to Calvin that Christ was put to death on a cross. The cross carried with it a divine curse; Christ bore the cross with its curse for sinful men and women:

> The form of Christ's death also embodies a singular mystery. The cross was accursed, not only in human opinion but by decree of God's law (Deut. 21:23). Hence, when Christ is hanged upon the cross, he makes himself subject to the curse. It had to happen in this way in order that the whole curse – which on account of our sins awaited us, or rather lay upon us – might be lifted from us, while it was transferred to him.[21]

The curse of the cross is the curse of the law, the threat of judgment, which the law announced to all law-breakers. Christ through his death redeemed sinners from the curse of the law:

> It is because He was made a curse that He might redeem us from the curse of the law, because He has revoked the power of the law, so far as it held us liable to the judgment of God under pain of eternal death, because, in a word, He has rescued us from the tyranny of sin, Satan, and death.[22]

Calvin is emphatic that Christ our legal substitute bore on the cross not only the judgment of Pilate, but also the full weight of divine judgment against sin. Calvin reveals the deepest reason for Christ's agony in Gethsemane's garden:

---

20. Cf. Calvin's commentary on John 1:29, and Boniface A. Willems and Reinhold Weier, *Soteriologie von der Reformation bis zur Gegenwart*, p. 27.
21. *Institutes* II. xvi. 6.
22. Calvin's commentary on Gal. 5:1. Cf. Calvin's commentaries on Luke 2:22 and Gal. 3:13. Stein has accurately explained Calvin's understanding of Christ's taking the curse of the law on the cross: 'He knows the curse-character of the law. What the law demands is for vacillating flesh an impossible, unattainable thing. No one is ready to

> It was not simple horror of death, the passing away from the world, but the sight of the dread tribunal of God that came to Him, the Judge Himself armed with vengeance beyond understanding. Our sins, whose burden was laid on Him, weighed on Him with their vast mass.[23]

In saying this Calvin wants to impress upon all Christians the great cost of their salvation. 'We must learn that death was no pastime or game to Christ, but that He was cast into the severest torments for our sake,' Calvin writes in his exegesis of John 12:27.[24] Commenting on the famous messianic passage, Isaiah 53, Calvin concludes, 'Thus the wrath of God, which had been justly kindled against us, was appeased.'[25]

If one were to ask Calvin to describe Christ's experience in bearing the burden of God's judgment, he would reply with the concept of estrangement, as he does in his commentary on Matthew 27:46:

> This was His chief conflict, harder than any other agony, that in His anguish He was not given relief by His Father's aid or favour, but made to feel somehow estranged. He does not only offer His body as the price of our reconciliation with God, but also in His soul He bore our due pains.[26]

---

bring complete love from his whole heart; no one is completely free from all lusts. The law thus makes us sinners worthy of death, not because of the guilt of Moses, but because we are depraved men who stand hostile to the command of God by virtue of our corrupt natures. This is the curse of the law: it demands relentlessly; it curses the disobedient; it punishes the conscience tyrannically and condemns it making it a slave. This curse Christ has taken to himself and borne on the cross. Through him who for us became a curse we have become free from the conscience-enslaving, dreadful, damning weight of the law'(Siegfried Stein, 'Mose und Christus bei Calvin', *Reformierte Kirchenzeitung* 88 [1938]: 197).

23. Calvin's commentary on Matt. 26:37.
24. Calvin's commentary on John 12:27.
25. Calvin's commentary on Isa 53:5.
26. Cf. Calvin's commentaries on Matt. 27:39 and Ps. 22:1.

It was in speaking of Christ's estrangement from God, his suffering in soul as well as in body, that Calvin's interpretation of the descent into hell had its deepest significance. Calvin warned his readers not to belittle Christ's descent:

> But we ought not to omit his descent into hell, a matter of no small moment in bringing about redemption.... If any persons have scruples about admitting this article into the Creed, it will soon be made plain how important it is to the sum of our redemption: if it is left out, much of the benefit of Christ's death will be lost.[27]

Christ made no journey to the nether world. Rather, he suffered God's judgment on the cross. The descent consisted of condemnation endured in body and soul:

> If Christ had died only a bodily death, it would have been ineffectual. No – it was expedient at the same time for him to undergo the severity of God's vengeance, to appease his wrath and satisfy his just judgment.... No wonder, then, if he is said to have descended into hell, for he suffered the death that God in his wrath had inflicted upon the wicked![28]

Calvin further interprets the descent in terms of estrangement:

> And surely no more terrible abyss can be conceived than to feel yourself forsaken and estranged from God; and when you call upon him, not to be heard. It is as if God himself had plotted your ruin. We see that Christ was so cast down as to be compelled to cry out in deep anguish: 'My God, my God, why hast thou forsaken me?' (Ps. 22:1).[29]

Calvin is not the first person to formulate the legal/penal view of the atonement. In fact, both Luther and Zwingli before him had

---

27. *Institutes* II. xvi. 8.
28. Ibid., II. xvi. 10. In *Institutes* II. xvi. 12, Calvin says, 'And surely, unless his soul shared in the punishment, he would have been the Redeemer of bodies alone.'
29. Ibid., II. xvi. 11.

taught it. 'But it belongs to Calvin to have given to the penal substitutionary doctrine of the atonement a compelling statement.'[30] According to Calvin's third theme of the atonement, Christ is our legal substitute who perfectly fulfills the law in his life and takes the condemnation law-breakers deserved in his death on the cross. This does not mean that Calvin has no use for the law in the life of the believer. On the contrary, Calvin affirms that the principle use of the law is as a rule of life for Christians.[31]

---

30. H. D. McDonald, 'Models of the Atonement in Reformed Theology,' in *Major Themes in the Reformed Tradition*, ed. Donald K. McKim (Eugene, Oregon: Wipf and Stock, 1998), 120. Not all agree. Some have argued that Calvin naively adopted the ideas of criminal law current in the reformation period when he devised his doctrine of penal substitution. On this basis Paul S. Fiddes, for example, faults Calvin's doctrine of Christ's penal suffering as being 'coloured by views of justice at the time'. Although no one is immune from cultural influence, Calvin included, I deem the reformer's view of penal substitution to be a better reflection of biblical teaching than Fiddes', whose thought seems adversely affected by late twentieth century therapeutic, personalist, and subjectivist concerns. Paul S. Fiddes, *Past Event and Present Salvation. The Christian Idea of Atonement* (Louisville: Westminster/ John Knox, 1989), pp. 97-104.
31. Calvin distinguishes three uses of the law in *Institutes* II. vii. 6-13: (1) to condemn sinners; (2) to regulate civil life; and (3) to serve as a guide for Christians. The second or civil use of the law does not concern us here. In its first use the law, 'warns, informs, convicts, and lastly condemns every man of his own unrighteousness' (ibid., II. vii. 6). The law thus is a condemnatory instrument. Calvin speaks of 'the rigor of the Law' (ibid., II. vii. 15). By this he means the threat of judgment, which the law pronounces upon unrepentant sinners. Believers in Christ are delivered from the rigor of the law, but they are never free from the claim of the law upon their lives. In *Institutes* II. vii. 12 Calvin explains: 'The third and principal use, which pertains more closely to the proper purpose of the law, finds its place among believers in whose hearts the Spirit of God already lives and reigns.... Here is the best instrument for them to learn more thoroughly each day the nature

of the Lord's will to which they aspire, and to confirm them in the understanding of it.' Calvin deplores those who reject the third use of the law: 'Certain ignorant persons, not understanding this distinction, rashly cast out the whole of Moses, and bid farewell to the two Tables of the Law' (ibid., II. vii. 13). Calvin warns us to 'banish this wicked thought from our minds.' He gives the reason: 'For Moses has admirably taught that the law, which among sinners can engender nothing but death, ought among the saints to have a better and more excellent use.' In fact, the law is 'a perfect pattern of righteousness ... one everlasting and unchangeable rule to live by ... applicable to every age, even to the end of the world' (ibid.).

7

CHRIST OUR SACRIFICE

'The sacrificial victims which were offered under the law to atone for sins were so called, not because they were capable of recovering God's favor or wiping out iniquity, but because they prefigured a true sacrifice such as was finally accomplished in reality by Christ alone; and by him alone, because no other could have done it. And it was done but once, because the effectiveness and force of that one sacrifice accomplished by Christ are eternal...; that is, whatever was necessary to recover the Father's favor, to obtain forgiveness of sins, righteousness, and salvation – all this was performed and completed by that unique sacrifice of his' (*Inst.* IV.xviii.13-14).

Jesus Christ died as an atoning sacrifice for the sins of his people. This sacrificial theme is one of Calvin's most important ways of viewing Christ's death. Although calling it 'the heart of Calvin's explication of the atonement', as Culpepper does, is an exaggeration,[1] it is one of three key atonement themes in Calvin's theology, along with the *Christus Victor* and legal themes. There is substantial overlapping between Christ's priestly office and the sacrificial theme of the atonement. There are, however, significant differences too, which justify including sacrifice as a separate theme of the atonement. The focus when discussing Christ's priestly office was on both the person and work of the Mediator. Here I will treat only the latter. In the chapter on the threefold office, both reconciliation and intercession were involved in Christ's priestly ministry. Now we are concerned only with the cross, and so intercession drops from view. Here belong important topics not dealt with in the discussion of Christ's priestly office: the Godward and manward aspects of Christ's

1. Robert H. Culpepper, *Interpreting the Atonement* (Grand Rapids: Eerdmans, 1966), p. 97.

sacrifice, and a study of Calvin's use of the major biblical words related to the atonement.

It is important to keep in mind the Old Testament background of Calvin's sacrificial theme of the atonement. Since this was dealt with in the treatment of Christ's priestly office, here only a brief review is needed.[2] Calvin's exposition of 1 Peter 1:19 emphasizes this Old Testament perspective of Christ's sacrifice:

> He means by this analogy that in Christ we have everything that has been foreshadowed by the ancient sacrifices, though he especially alludes to the Paschal Lamb.... By applying this to Christ Peter teaches us that He was a suitable victim, approved by God, for He was perfect, without any blemish. Had He had any defect in Him, He could not have been rightly offered to God, nor could He pacify His wrath.[3]

Christ came in fulfillment of the Old Testament predictions and types. He is 'the Lamb of God who takes away the sin of the world' (John 1:29). Calvin's comments on this verse make clear that Christ's death is the great and final sacrifice for sin:

> The chief office of Christ is explained briefly but clearly. By taking away the sins of the world by the sacrifice of His death, He reconciles men to God. Christ certainly bestows other blessings upon us, but the chief one, on which all the others depend, is that by appeasing the wrath of God He brings it to pass that we are reckoned righteous and pure.... by not imputing our sins, God receives us into favour.... Therefore, John, putting Christ forward, bears witness that He is the Lamb of God; by which he means that whatever sacrificial victims

---

2. Chapter 3, pp. 54-58. Schellong is correct when he claims that Calvin relies heavily on Isa. 53 in his presentation of Christ's death as a sacrifice (Dieter Schellong, *Calvins Auslegung der synoptischen Evangelien*, p. 278). I concur with Paul, who notes that sufficient attention has not been given to Calvin's treatment of the Old Testament sacrifices in the light of his sacrificial picture of Christ's work (Robert S. Paul, *The Atonement and the Sacraments*, p. 101).
3. Calvin's commentary on 1 Pet. 1:19.

the Jews used to offer under the Law had no power at all to atone for sins, but were only figures whose reality was revealed in Christ Himself.[4]

Christ died as an expiatory victim in the place of sinners. Substitution is prominent in Calvin's presentation of Christ's sacrifice. Commenting on Isaiah 53:10, 'If He would render himself as a guilt offering...,' Calvin speaks of Christ as a sacrificial substitute who expiates the sins of his people and reconciles God to man:

> ...*asham* denotes both sin and the sacrifice which is offered for sin, and is used in the latter sense in the Scriptures. The sacrifice was offered in such a manner as to expiate sin by enduring its punishment and curse. This was expressed by the priests by means of the laying on of hands, as if they threw on the sacrifice the sins of the whole nation. And if a private individual offered a sacrifice, he also laid his hand upon it, as upon Christ in such a manner that he alone bore the curse.... What Paul meant by the words 'curse' and 'sin' in these passages is the same as what the prophet meant by the word...*asham*. In short...*asham* is equivalent to the Latin word *piaculum*, an expiatory sacrifice.... Here we have a description of the benefit of Christ's death, that by his sacrifice sins were expiated, and God was reconciled towards men; for such is the import of the word...*asham*.[5]

Calvin has much to say about the 'blood' of Christ. His exegesis of Hebrews 9:22 underscores that Christ's blood is 'the sacrifice of His death': 'Just as there is neither purity nor salvation apart from Christ, so nothing could be either pure or saving without blood because Christ must never be separated from the sacrifice of His death.'[6] The importance of Christ's blood is shown by its occasional use in Scripture as a synecdochical reference to the

---

4. Calvin's commentary on John 1:29.
5. Cf. Calvin's commentaries on John 19:17 and Rom. 8:3.
6. Calvin's commentary on Heb. 9:22. Cf. Calvin's commentaries on Col. 1:20 and 1 John 5:6.

whole redemptive process with all its parts:

> By mentioning blood alone he did not mean to exclude other parts of redemption, but rather to include the whole of it in a single word, and he mentioned the blood, in which we are washed. Thus, the whole of our expiation is denoted by taking a part for the whole.[7]

Calvin's presentation of Christ's sacrifice includes both Godward and manward aspects. In the *Institutes*, Calvin writes, 'He offered as a sacrifice the flesh he received from us, that he might wipe out our guilt by his act of expiation and appease the Father's righteous wrath.'[8] Here Christ's sacrifice is directed toward God (appeasing his wrath) and toward man (wiping out his guilt). The same two aspects of Christ's work are reflected in Calvin's comments on Matthew 16:16:

> In the praise of Christ is comprehended His eternal kingdom and priesthood, that he reconciles God to us and wins perfect righteousness, expiating our sins by His sacrifice, that He keeps His own, whom He has received into His trust and care, and adorns and enriches us with every kind of blessing.[9]

Some have sought to stress the manward aspect of Christ's sacrifice in Calvin to the downplaying of the Godward.[10] This can be done only with injury to Calvin's thought. Santmire's summary captures better the balanced approach of Calvin:

> Although Calvin does not distinguish the words, his Atonement doctrine contains both the ideas of propitiation and expiation; the former here being understood as the appeasement of the offended divine majesty or satisfaction, the latter being understood as the covering over or, as Calvin sometimes says, the purging of the sin of

---

7. Calvin's commentary on Rom. 3:25.
8. *Institutes* II. xii. 3.
9. Calvin's commentary on Matt. 16:16.
10. Cf. Brian A. Gerrish, 'Atonement and "Saving Faith",' *Theology Today* 17 (1960-61): 187ff.

> the creature.... Christ's death thus has a vertical or a theocentric reference on the one hand and a horizontal or an anthropocentric reference on the other hand.[11]

The New Testament contains many words relating to the atonement: propitiation, reconciliation, redemption, etc. Calvin applies these biblical words to his sacrificial theme of Christ's work:

> But that these things may take root firmly and deeply in our hearts, let us keep sacrifice and cleansing constantly in mind. For we could not believe with assurance that Christ is our redemption, ransom, and propitiation unless he had been a sacrificial victim. Blood is accordingly mentioned whenever Scripture discusses the mode of redemption. Yet Christ's shed blood served, not only as a satisfaction, but also as a laver to wash away our corruption.[12]

It is good to examine three of these biblical words as understood by Calvin in terms of the direction of Christ's sacrificial death: toward God (propitiation), toward human beings (redemption), and toward God and men (reconciliation). Christ's death is a propitiation that turns away the wrath of a holy God. Referring to 1 John 2:1f. ('Jesus Christ ... and He Himself is the propitiation for our sins', NASB) Calvin explains in the *Institutes*, '... while he sets forth Christ as the propitiation of sins, he shows that there is no other satisfaction whereby offended God can be propitiated or appeased.'[13] That Calvin understands propitiation in sacrificial terms is evident from his exposition of 1 John 2:1:

> Propitiation is put in, because none is fit to be the High Priest without a sacrifice. Thus, under the law, the priest never entered the sanctuary without blood having been shed; and according to God's appointment, it was the custom for a sacrifice to accompany prayers as the usual

11. H. Paul Santmire, 'Justification in Calvin's 1540 Romans Commentary', *Church History* 33 (1964): 299f.
12. *Institutes* II. xvi. 6.
13. Ibid., III. iv. 26.

> seal. By this symbol God wanted to show that he who procures grace for us must be furnished with a sacrifice. For when God is offended, the price of a satisfaction is required to pacify Him.[14]

Thus for Calvin propitiation is that aspect of Christ's sacrifice by which God's holy anger against sin is satisfied and turned away. The Son of God stepped into the place of sinners and bore the brunt of God's wrath against their sins.

Closely related to propitiation in Calvin's thought is the biblical concept of reconciliation. The background is enmity: since God is angry at sinners because of their sins, they are not at peace with him. Sin constitutes a real barrier between God and sinners. Christ through his sacrificial death removed the barrier from God's side, reconciling him to his people: 'For ye were "alienated"; that is, from God. Ye were "enemies"; now ye are received into favour. Whence comes this? It is because God, appeased by the death of Christ has become reconciled to you.'[15]

On the other hand, believers are reconciled to God through Christ when they personally trust in him as their sacrifice; 'Let us therefore learn that we are reconciled to God by the grace of Christ if we go straight to His death and believe that He was nailed to the cross as the only sacrificial victim by whom all our guilt is removed.'[16] This quotation brings out well the sacrificial coloring of reconciliation in Calvin. Whereas before reconciliation God was our judge, now 'we know that God is our merciful Father, because of reconciliation effected through Christ'.[17] Reconciliation, therefore, operates in two directions. We sinners are reconciled to God through the death of Christ, our peacemaker. In addition, reconciliation is an aspect of Christ's sacrificial work in Calvin's thought that is directed toward God: God is both reconciled to sinners and propitiated through the sacrifice of his Son.

---

14. Calvin's commentary on 1 John 2:1. Cf. Calvin's commentary on Matt. 26:3.
15. Calvin's commentary on Col. 1:21.
16. Calvin's commentary on John 1:29.
17. *Institutes* III. ii. 2.

Calvin also conceived of the work of Christ our sacrifice as directed towards human beings. The biblical word 'redemption' is connected with this. The background of this word is bondage; before knowing Christ, sinners were in 'slavery to sin', which brought them 'all the misery which flows from it'. Christ redeems his people, that is, he delivers them from bondage to sin: 'Paul teaches that he was given to us for Redemption. By that he means that we are delivered by His goodness from all slavery to sin, and from all the misery which flows from it.... He made Himself the price of redemption.'[18]

Redemption, as the end of the previous quotation reveals, involves the payment of a price. In *Institutes* II. xvii. 5, Calvin tells what the price of redemption was:

> The apostles clearly state that he paid the price to redeem us from the penalty of death, 'being justified ... by his grace through the redemption that is in Christ ... whom God put forward as a propitiation through faith which is in his blood' (Rom. 3:24-25). Paul commends God's grace in this respect: for God has given the price of redemption in the death of Christ (Rom. 3:24).[19]

Redemption stresses the fact that Christ's sacrificial death was directed towards us – believers are redeemed through his blood. At the same time redemption is objective because Christ's death is the redemption price paid to deliver Christians from sin's power. The fruit of redemption is the liberty of the children of God; there is a resultant state of freedom into which believers are redeemed. In his commentary on Titus, Calvin writes: 'Christ offered Himself for us that He might redeem us from slavery to sin and purchase us for Himself as His possession.'[20]

It remains to consider the efficacy of Christ's sacrifice on the cross. Calvin labels its efficacy 'perpetual' and assures his readers that 'it extends to all ages'. Thus Old Testament saints

---

18. Calvin's commentary on 1 Cor. 1:30.
19. Cf. Calvin's commentary on Mark 10:45.
20. Calvin's commentary on Titus 2:14.

were forgiven only in anticipation of Christ's perfect sacrifice for sin:

> Since that one sacrifice which Christ offered once for all has eternal power, and is therefore perpetual in its efficacy, it is no wonder that the eternal priesthood of Christ is supported by its power which never fails.... The power of the one sacrifice is eternal and extends to all ages.... Therefore unless the sacrifice of Christ was efficacious, none of the fathers would have obtained salvation. Since in themselves they were subject to the wrath of God, they had no remedy to deliver them had it not been that Christ by suffering once for all suffered what was necessary to reconcile men to the grace of God from the beginning of the world right to the end.[21]

The great power of Christ's sacrifice guarantees believers' safety in Christ; God who saved them will keep them saved through the sacrifice of his Son: 'Therefore let it remain a determined principle that the righteousness which we are given in Christ is not the thing of a single day or a moment, but is permanent, so that the sacrifice of His death daily reconciles us to God.'[22]

It is in the context of the efficacy of Christ's sacrifice that Calvin takes great affront at the Roman Catholic mass. In the *Institutes*, he explains:

> The sacrificial victims which were offered under the law to atone for sins were so called, not because they were capable of recovering God's favor or wiping out iniquity, but because they prefigured a true sacrifice such as was finally accomplished in reality by Christ alone; and by him alone, because no other could have done it. And it was done but once, because the effectiveness and force of that one sacrifice accomplished by Christ are eternal, as he testified with his own voice when he said that it was done and fulfilled; that is, whatever was necessary to recover the Father's favor, to obtain forgiveness of sins, righteousness, and salvation – all this was performed and completed by that unique sacrifice of his. And so perfect was it that

---

21. Calvin's commentary on Heb. 9:25f.
22. Calvin's commentary on Acts 13:39.

> no place was left afterward for any other sacrificial victim. Therefore, I conclude that it is a most wicked infamy and unbearable blasphemy, both against Christ and against the sacrifice which he made for us through his death on the cross, for anyone to suppose that by repeating the oblation he obtains pardon for sins, appeases God, and acquires righteousness. But what else is done by performing masses except that by the merit of a new oblation we are made partakers in Christ's passion?[23]

Calvin regards the mass as an insult to the sacrifice of Christ. Christ offered up his body and blood on the cross as the final sacrifice for sin. To perform any other priestly sacrifices after Christ's death is to impugn the accomplishment of his perfect sacrifice. In Calvin's eyes, to perform a mass was to say that Christ's work was not sufficient to put away sins. Masses are attempts to add to the sacrifice of Christ as if something were lacking. But Christ's work was perfect and no other sacrifices are needed. Christ perfectly fulfilled the Old Testament sacrificial system by offering himself on the cross. His work is sufficient to save his people from their sins. To perform a mass is to disregard the sacrifice of Christ and to attempt to appease God by other means.

This is Calvin's fourth theme of the atonement: Christ offers himself as a sacrifice on the cross in the place of sinners to propitiate God's wrath and reconcile him to them, and to redeem them from bondage to sin and reconcile them to God.

---

23. *Institutes* IV. xviii. 13-14.

8

CHRIST OUR MERIT

'By his obedience, however, Christ truly acquired and merited grace for us with his Father. Many passages of Scripture surely and firmly attest this. I take it to be commonplace that if Christ made satisfaction for our sins, if he paid the penalty owed by us, if he appeased God by his obedience – in short, if as a righteous man he suffered for unrighteous men – then he acquired salvation for us by his righteousness, which is tantamount to deserving it' (*Inst.* II. xvii. 3).

Jesus Christ redeems his people not only by taking away their sins, but also by meriting grace and salvation for them. This is Calvin's atonement theme of Christ our merit. Although the idea of Christ meriting salvation for Christians was present in previous editions of the *Institutes*, it is only in the 1559 (final) edition that Calvin devotes a chapter to the topic (II. xvii). As a result of correspondence and debate with Laelius Socinus, 'Calvin was forced to give expanded clarification to the doctrine of the merit of Christ.'[1] Socinus' letters are not extant, and so we must reconstruct his side of the discussion from Calvin's writings. At the very beginning of *Institutes* II. xvii, Calvin alludes to Socinus when he says: 'By way of addition this question also should be explained. There are certain perversely subtle men who – even though they confess that we receive salvation through Christ –

1. E. David Willis, 'The Influence of Laelius Socinus on Calvin's Doctrines of the Merits of Christ and the Assurance of Faith', in *Italian Reformation Studies in Honor of Laelius Socinus*, ed. John A. Tedeschi (Firenze: Le Monnier, 1965), p. 236. This article provides an outstanding summary of the 1555 correspondence in which Calvin answers four questions directed to him by Laelius Socinus dealing with the merits of Christ and assurance.

cannot bear to hear the word "merit", for they think that it obscures God's grace.'[2]

Socinus is asking a question about the faithfulness of God. Can we count on God's faithfulness 'if his will is mutable as would seem to be implied by a doctrine of the merits of Christ'?[3] Socinus struggles with two seemingly irreconcilable ideas. How can redemption be of God's free mercy and yet Christ merit grace and salvation for believers? How can God's forgiveness be free and at the same time Christ merit it for his own?

Calvin's replies to these questions in *Institutes* II. xvii form a good starting point for a discussion of Christ our merit. Calvin responds to Socinus by claiming that 'God's mercy and Christ's merit are not in opposition'. One must distinguish between first and second causes:

> In discussing Christ's merit, we do not consider the beginning of merit to be in him, but we go back to God's ordinance, the first cause. For God solely of his own good pleasure appointed him Mediator to obtain salvation for us. Hence it is absurd to set Christ's merit against God's mercy. For it is a common rule that a thing subordinate to another is not in conflict with it. For this reason nothing hinders us from asserting that men are freely justified by God's mercy alone, and at the same time that Christ's merit, subordinate to God's mercy, also intervenes on our behalf.[4]

God's love is the first cause of salvation. Christ, however, truly merited grace and salvation for his people. This was the subordinate cause, God's means of bringing his love to believers.

Socinus stumbles because he sets the wrong ideas in opposition. In *Institutes* II. xvii. 1, Calvin seeks to correct him:

---

2. *Institutes* II. xvii. 1.
3. Willis, 'The Influence of Laelius Socinus', p. 234.
4. *Institutes* II. xvii. 1. Willis sums up the matter well: 'Calvin answers that it is by Christ's merits that the Father who has always loved us and who is now reconciled to us embraces us and discloses his love' (Willis, 'The Influence of Laelius Socinus', p. 234).

> Both God's free favor and Christ's obedience, each in its degree, are fitly opposed to our works. Apart from God's good pleasure Christ could not merit anything; but did so because he had been appointed to appease God's wrath with his sacrifice, and to blot out our transgressions with his obedience. To sum up: inasmuch as Christ's merit depends upon God's grace alone, which has ordained this manner of salvation for us, it is just as properly opposed to all human righteousness as God's grace is.[5]

Socinus errs because he fails to see Christ's merit as God's ordained means of procuring salvation. Calvin accuses Socinus of perverse speculation in departing from the Word of God. The duty of a Christian theologian is humbly to receive the teaching of Holy Scripture; it is not creatively to manipulate Christian doctrine according to one's fancy. To Calvin, Socinus' speculations about God's freedom, apart from the historical revelation of God's will in the Mediator, are dangerous.[6]

Calvin is emphatic that Christ merited grace and salvation for his people:

> By his obedience, however, Christ truly acquired and merited grace for us with his Father. Many passages of Scripture surely and firmly attest this. I take it to be commonplace that if Christ made satisfaction for our sins, if he paid the penalty owed by us, if he appeased God by his obedience – in short, if as a righteous man he suffered for

---

5. Willis is correct when he writes with reference to Calvin's reply to Socinus: 'According to this answer the basic opposition is not between God's free favor and Christ's obedience, but between God's saving action, including his free favor and Christ's obedience, and our works. Men cannot merit what flows from Christ's obedience' (Willis, 'The Influence of Laelius Socinus', p. 235).
6. *Institutes* II. xvii. 1. Willis sums up Calvin's doctrine of the merits of Christ: 'Such a doctrine of Christ's merits is based on a refusal to take seriously an abstract notion of God's freedom apart from its manifestation in the Redeemer's fulfillment of the will of the Father in an obedience which eventually meant the death on the cross' (Willis, 'The Influence of Laelius Socinus', p. 235).

> unrighteous men – then he acquired salvation for us by his righteousness, which is tantamount to deserving it.[7]

God the Father is the ultimate fount of saving grace. Yet Christ also is a source of grace for his people. He merited this grace for all believers: 'From this it follows that Christ bestows on us something of what he has acquired. For otherwise it would not be fitting for this credit to be given to him as distinct from the Father, namely that grace is his and proceeds from him.'[8]

Sometimes when speaking of Christ our merit, Calvin employs legal terminology. That is just one illustration of the fact that Calvin's themes of the atonement are not in watertight compartments; there is an overlap between them. Here Christ's meriting salvation overlaps the 'active obedience' of the picture of Christ our legal substitute. In the *Institutes*, Calvin teaches:

> From this we infer that we must seek from Christ what the law would give if anyone could fulfill it; or, what is the same thing, that we obtain through Christ's grace what God promised in the law for our works.... For if righteousness consists in the observance of the law, who will deny that Christ merited favor for us, when, by taking that burden upon himself, he reconciled us to God as if we had kept the law?... What was the purpose of this subjection of Christ to the law but to acquire righteousness for us, undertaking to pay what we could not pay?[9]

This theme of the work of Christ involves his whole earthly life of obedience. Yet the idea of Christ acquiring merit for his people in no way is to be separated from his death on the cross. It is by his death too that Jesus Christ merits grace for believers. Throughout *Institutes* II. xvii. 4-5 Calvin makes this clear:

> But when we say that grace was imparted to us by the merit of Christ, we mean this: by his blood we were cleansed, and his death was an expiation for our sins.... If the effect of his shedding of blood

7. *Institutes* II. xvii. 3.
8. Ibid., II. xvii. 2.
9. Ibid., II. xvii. 5.

> is that our sins are not imputed to us, it follows that God's judgment was satisfied by that price.... This readily shows that Christ's grace is much weakened unless we grant to his sacrifice the power of expiating, appeasing, and making satisfaction.... The apostles clearly state that he paid the price to redeem us from the penalty of death.... the Son of God was crucified as the price of our righteousness.[10]

Via this atonement motif Calvin stresses the positive achievement of salvation by Christ on behalf of his people. Calvin affirms that Christ is the author of salvation: '... certain perversely subtle men ... cannot bear to hear the word "merit", for they think that it obscures God's grace. Hence, they would have Christ as a mere

---

10. Scholars have noted the similarity between Calvin's view of Christ's merits and that of Duns Scotus. Willis notes: 'The resemblance between Calvin's argument on the merits of Christ and that of Duns Scotus on the same subject has been noted and is indisputable. Both argue that apart from God's good pleasure, Christ could not merit anything. Scotus says that Christ's work and especially his willing was meritorious because of the *acceptio* of God' (Willis, 'The Influence of Laelius Socinus', pp. 235f). Here, however, the paths of Duns Scotus and Calvin diverge, for Scotus holds, 'If it had pleased God, a good angel could have made satisfaction by an offering which God could have accepted as sufficient for all sins. For every created offering is worth exactly what God accepts it for and no more' (ibid.). There are similarities between the ideas of Scotus and Calvin, but important differences too: 'Scotus, in the traditional fashion of Lombard, St. Thomas, and Bonaventura, considers both what Christ merited for himself and what he merited for others. Calvin restricts himself to what Christ merits for others. Scotus says that Christ's superabundant merit is indispensable, but not entirely sufficient for our salvation. For Calvin, Christ's merit means exactly that no merit is required or can be offered to supplement or complete Christ's deserving' (ibid.). In *Institutes* II. xvii. 6 Calvin repudiates the notion of Christ gaining merit for Himself as 'stupid curiosity'. On the contrary, 'he who gave away the fruit of his holiness to others testifies that he acquired nothing for himself.' Calvin affirms substitution when he speaks of Christ our merit. Scotus is more speculative and opens the door to the possibility of someone else meriting grace for us (cf. Willis, 'The Influence of Laelius Socinus', p. 236).

instrument or minister, not as the Author or leader and prince of life, as Peter calls him (Acts 3:15).'[11] By saying that Christ merited salvation, Calvin means that Christ is the material cause of salvation – he actually rescues believers by his righteousness:

> Suppose someone takes exception that Christ is only a formal cause. He then diminishes Christ's power more than the words just quoted bear out. For if we attain righteousness by a faith that reposes in him, we ought to seek the matter of our salvation in him.[12]

Some of Calvin's other pictures of reconciliation portray the 'negative' aspects of redemption. Christ received condemnation as his people's legal substitute. He offered himself as the atoning sacrifice for sin. He vanquished believers' foes as the mighty victor. The theme of Christ our merit, however, sets forth in *positive* terms the way Jesus Christ redeemed sinners: he merited grace and salvation for them.

---

11. *Institutes* II. xvii. 1.
12. Ibid., II. xvii. 2. Van Buren accurately presents Calvin's view when he says, '"Christ is correctly and fittingly said to have merited the grace of God and salvation for us." It is the word "merit" that he wishes to stress, for it excludes every attempt to make the work of Christ merely instrumental to our salvation' (Paul Van Buren, *Christ in Our Place*, p. 61).

9

CHRIST OUR EXAMPLE

'The words should be resolved like this: "If any one wished to be mine, when he has denied himself and taken up his cross, let him follow me", or, "let him conform to my example" – meaning that none can be considered Christ's disciple who is not a true imitator of Him and prepared to run the same course' (Calvin's Commentary on Matthew 16:24).

Calvin's final theme of the atonement presents Christ in his death as an example to Christians. There is an important difference between this motif and the five others that have been examined. Each of those deals primarily with the way we become Christians. The exemplary theme relates not to initial salvation, but to the way we are to live the Christian life. In Calvin's first chapter on the Christian life in the *Institutes*, he says: '... Christ through whom we return into favor with God, has been set before us as an example, whose pattern we ought to express in our life.'[1] Christ is first of all 'He through whom we return into favor with God.' Then he is also a pattern for Christian living. Make careful note – Christ as example is for disciples only: 'But it behoves the godly mind to climb still higher, to the height to which Christ calls his disciples: That each must bear his own cross (Matt. 16:24).'[2]

Some have failed to see the way Calvin correlates the exemplary picture of the atonement to the Christian life rather than to initial salvation and reject the concept of Christ being an example in his death.[3] Calvin, however, finds an exemplary theme

---

1. *Institutes* III. vi. 3.
2. Ibid., III. viii. 1.
3. Jansen, for example, finds in Calvin nothing of Christ as an example in his death: 'Nowhere does he relate the prophetic office to the Cross. Indeed, it seems that Calvin sees a peril in trying to do so – for an

of the atonement in the New Testament. He understands that this theme was never presented as the way to salvation, but was always a part of the Christian life. Thus he asks: 'Why should we exempt ourselves, therefore, from the condition to which Christ our Head had to submit, especially since he submitted to it for our sake to show us an example of patience in himself.'[4] Rather, 'He invites each member of His Body to imitate Him.'[5] Calvin is very clear – Christ is an example for Christians only, for those who have been brought into spiritual union with Christ and who are thus members of his body, the church. In his exposition of 1 Peter 2:23 Calvin demonstrates the systematic carefulness that is characteristic of him:

> If he had commended nothing in Christ's death except its example, he would have been too narrow in his view, and he now refers to a much more excellent fruit. There are three things to be noticed in this passage. The first is that by His death Christ has given us an example of patience; the second, that by His death He has redeemed and restored us to life; for which it follows that we are so bound to Him, that we ought gladly to follow His example. In the third place, he refers to the general purpose of His death, that we, being dead to sins, ought to live in righteousness.[6]

Christ as an example in his death forms an important part of Calvin's doctrine of the Christian life. Calvin's understanding of Matthew 16:24 ('Then Jesus said to His disciples, "If any one

---

exemplary theory of atonement takes from the Cross its objective and saving character' (John F. Jansen, *Calvin's Doctrine of the Work of Christ*, p. 58). Wallace sets the context for Calvin's use of the picture of Christ our example: 'When Calvin speaks of our conformity to the pattern of Jesus Christ, it is usually in the context of union between the Head and members of the body. It is within the relationship of union with Christ that we are exhorted to imitate Christ as our example' (Ronald S. Wallace, *Calvin's Doctrine of the Christian Life*, p. 47).

4. *Institutes* III. viii. 1.
5. Calvin's commentary on Matt. 16:24.
6. Calvin's commentary on 1 Pet. 2:23.

wishes to come after Me, let him deny himself, and take up his cross, and follow Me'") is determinative for his theological ethics. The titles of two of his most important chapters in the *Institutes* on the Christian life bear this out: 'The Sum of the Christian Life: The Denial of Ourselves' (III. vii), and 'Bearing the Cross, a Part of Self-denial' (III. viii). In his commentary on Matthew 16:24 Calvin paraphrases the words of Christ:

> The words should be resolved like this: 'If any one wished to be mine, when he has denied himself and taken up his cross, let him follow me', or, 'let him conform to my example' – meaning that none can be considered Christ's disciple who is not a true imitator of Him and prepared to run the same course.[7]

There are other aspects to Calvin's doctrine of the Christian life: meditation on the future life, thanksgiving, stewardship, etc. But none of these is more important than self-denial.

Calvin calls Christians to an exercise of caution as they look about for models to follow. He does not deny that believers are to imitate the lives of other godly Christians. Yet there is a higher standard to which Christian models must conform if they are to

---

7. Niesel underlined the importance of Matt. 16:24 for Calvin's ethical thought: 'But by taking as his starting point for ethics the insight that we are called to imitate Christ, he makes quite clear the ultimate aim of the commands of the law.

'Only those can be called disciples of Christ who truly imitate him and are prepared to follow in his footsteps. He has given us a summary rule of discipleship so that we may know in what the imitation of him essentially consists: namely, self-denial and the willing bearing of his cross. Thus in surveying the Christian life from these two points of view, self-denial and the bearing of the cross, he is holding fast to the rule of discipleship which Christ himself has given us in Matt. 16:24. In both passages of the *Institutes* he expressly refers to this word of the Lord. What he says is nothing more than an exposition of this word of Christ. If we fail to see this and try to explain Calvin's arguments in a different sense, we do not understand them at all' (Wilhelm Niesel, *The Theology of Calvin*, p. 143).

serve as examples for God's people. Speaking of the apostle Paul, Calvin comments: '... he points himself and others back to Christ as the one exemplar of right action ... we are only to follow men, provided that they have Christ as their prototype.'[8] Christians must not even follow the Lord's example willy-nilly. Believers must distinguish between actions of his that are their objects of imitation and those not intended to be. Commenting on John 13:14, Calvin explains:

> It is to be noted also that Christ says that He gave an example. For it is not right to take all His actions indiscriminately as objects of imitation. The Papists boast that they follow Christ's example in keeping the Lenten fast. But we must first see whether or no He intended to put forward an example as a norm for disciples to conform to. We read nothing of the sort.[9]

Calvin holds that Jesus Christ is an example in his death in many different areas. Before one investigates these areas it must be kept in mind that they do not exhaust Calvin's teaching on the *imitatio Christi*. Although Calvin affirmed that Christ was an example in his life, the focus here is only on Christ's example in his death.

As believers face temptations they can bolster their hearts with the knowledge that the Lord was tempted when 'He endured a bitter death'. Calvin's comments on Hebrews 12:3 bear this out:

> This thought alone ought to be sufficient to conquer all temptation, when we realise that we are the companions of the Son of God and that He who was so far above us was willing to come down to our condition to encourage us by His example.[10]

---

8. Calvin's commentary on 1 Cor. 11:1.
9. Calvin's commentary on John 13:14. Cf. Ronald S. Wallace, *Calvin's Doctrine of the Christian Life*, pp. 42f.
10. Calvin's commentary on Heb. 12:3. Cf. Max Dominicé, *L'humanité de Jésus d'après Calvin*, p. 213.

In his exegesis of 1 Peter 2:21ff., the *textus classicus* for the exemplary theme of the atonement, Calvin presents Jesus in his death as an example of patiently bearing unjust suffering:

> ... he consoles us with the example of Christ. Nothing seems more unworthy, and therefore less tolerable, than undeservedly to suffer, but when we turn our eyes to the Son of God, this bitterness is mitigated, for who would refuse to follow Him as He goes before us?... Here Peter points out what we ought to imitate in Christ, to wit, that we should calmly bear wrongs, and not think of avenging them, for such is our disposition that when we receive injuries, our minds immediately boil over with the desire for revenge. But Christ abstained from every kind of retaliation. Our minds, therefore, ought to be bridled, so that we should not seek to render evil for evil.[11]

Moreover, Christ is the model of humility for believers:

> Rather does He form us to the imitation of Him, since we, in the obstinacy of our flesh, fly from His yoke as something harsh and difficult.... For, having exhorted His disciples to bear their Cross, Christ at once goes on, in case the difficulty should frighten them: 'Learn of me.' He means that the yoke will not be troublesome to them when they have become used to meekness and humility by His example.[12]

His death is also a pattern of love, as Calvin notes in his commentary on 2 Corinthians:

> Having mentioned love he now refers to Christ as the perfect and unique pattern of it. 'When He was rich,' he says, 'He gave up possession of all His blessings that He might enrich us by His poverty'.... Christ was rich because He was God.... But He became poor because He gave up His possession (of all things as heir) and for a time did not exercise His right (of dominion).[13]

---

11. Calvin's commentary on 1 Pet. 2:21ff.
12. Calvin's commentary on Matt. 11:29.
13. Calvin's commentary on 2 Cor. 8:9.

Husbands are especially singled out and called to follow Christ's example of love, as Calvin notes concerning Ephesians 5:25: 'Let husbands imitate Christ in this respect, that He did not hesitate to die for the Church.'[14]

In addition, Calvin holds forth Christ's praying for his enemies on the cross as an example of moderation:

> Moderation of this kind is the example Luke here gives in the Person of our Leader and Master, for when He might have called down a curse on His persecutors, to their ruin, He not only checked Himself from cursing but actually prayed for their good.[15]

If someone were to ask John Calvin to summarize the Christian life in one word, his answer would be *obedience*. Jesus Christ in dying is an example of obedience, as Calvin affirms in his commentary on Hebrews 5:8:

> He was more than willing of His own accord to give the Father the obedience due to Him. He did this for our benefit, to give us the instance and the pattern of His own submission even to death itself, although this can be said with truth, that it was in His death that Christ fully learned what it meant to obey God, since that was the point at which He reached His greatest self-denial. He renounced His own will and gave Himself over to the Father to the extent of meeting death, which He dreaded, freely and willingly. The meaning is, therefore, that by the experience of His sufferings Christ was taught how far we ought to submit to and obey God. Therefore we also should be instructed and guided into obedience to God by His example....[16]

The goal of the Christian life, according to Calvin, is to glorify God. The Savior, in going to the cross, exemplifies that goal:

> He testifies by these words that He puts the glory of the Father before everything else and disregards and neglects even His own

14. Calvin's commentary on Eph. 5:25.
15. Calvin's commentary on Luke 23:34.
16. Cf. Dominicé, p. 153.

> life. And the true regulating of our desires is so to seek God's glory that all the rest gives place to it. For we should regard it as abundant reward, that we may with a quiet mind bear all that is troublesome and irksome.[17]

Calvin's final theme of the atonement is one oriented entirely toward the Christian life: Christ is our example and Christians are called to imitate him in all that they think, say, and do.[18]

---

17. Calvin's commentary on John 12:28.
18. This chapter must be placed within the larger context of Calvin's doctrine of the Christian life. Calvin maintains that the dynamic for following Christ's example and obeying the law is the power of God working in Christians. In *Institutes* III. viii. 2 he teaches: 'He can best restrain this arrogance when he proves to us by experience not only the great incapacity but also the frailty under which we labor. Therefore, he afflicts us either with disgrace or poverty, or bereavement, or disease, or other calamities. Utterly unequal to bearing these, in so far as they touch us, we soon succumb to them. Thus humbled, we learn to call upon his power, which alone makes us stand fast under the weight of afflictions.'

10

CONCLUSION

'Fundamental to the doctrine of faith in John Calvin (1509-64) is his belief that Christ died indiscriminately for all men.... Had not Christ died for *all*, we could have no assurance that *our* sins have been expiated in God's sight....'[1]

'The evidence that Calvin was a limited redemptionist is far more extensive than the few quotations offered by writers like Murray and Helm... would indicate. There is... a wealth of explicit and unambiguous statements in Calvin to the effect that Christ died only for the elect....'[2]

'Well, what *was* Calvin's view?' This is a question I have frequently been asked when people learn that I studied Calvin's doctrine of the atonement. They are asking, of course, whether Calvin subscribed to a doctrine of limited atonement, the view that Christ died only to save the elect, or unlimited atonement, the view that he died to save everyone. As the quotations above demonstrate, scholars have strong and contrary opinions on this matter.

I will address Calvin's view of the extent of the atonement at the beginning of my conclusion for two reasons. First, because there continues to be great interest in the subject. Of the twenty-two Calvin sources that I added to the bibliography for this edition, half deal with this issue. Second, I will discuss Calvin on the extent of the atonement, an issue he does *not* address in the *Institutes*, because after having dealt with this issue, we will be

---

1. R. T. Kendall, *Calvin and English Calvinism to 1649* (Carlisle, Cumbria: Paternoster, 1979, 1997), pp. 13-14 (italics in original).
2. Jonathan Rainbow, 'Redemptor Ecclesiae, Redemptor Mundi: An Historical and Theological Study of John Calvin's Doctrine of the Extent of Redemption' (Ph.D. dissertation, University of California, Santa Barbara, 1986), p. 159.

able to focus on the many things he *does* address in the *Institutes* concerning the work of Christ.

There are three positions on Calvin's view of the extent of the atonement. Many insist that Calvin teaches unlimited atonement.[3] Others are equally insistent that Calvin holds to a limited atonement.[4] A few maintain that we cannot know for certain.[5]

Roger Nicole, who favors limited atonement in Calvin, cites Curt Daniel, who takes the opposite view, when Nicole admits a tendency of scholars to read their views into Calvin.

> 'Daniel makes a comment to the effect that most of the contenders in this area tend to ascribe to Calvin the view which they hold themselves, that is to say, they appear to have yielded to the temptation to annex Calvin in support of their own position! Unfortunately this remark seems to apply also to Daniel's treatment and to the present article.'[6]

Nicole's frankness is refreshing. Most *do* read their view of the extent of the atonement into Calvin.

It would be a mistake, however, for readers to conclude that people reach their conclusions on Calvin's view of the extent of

---

3. Paul Van Buren, *Christ in Our Place*, p. 50. Extensive work was done by James W. Anderson, 'The Grace of God and the Non-elect in Calvin's Commentaries and Sermons' (Th.D. dissertation, New Orleans Baptist Theological Seminary, 1976). He concludes in favor of unlimited atonement in Calvin largely on the basis of his sermons.
4. So A. A. Hodge, *The Atonement* (1867; reprinted, Grand Rapids: Eerdmans, 1953), pp. 388-91, and W. Robert Godfrey, 'Reformed Thought on the Extent of the Atonement to 1618', *Westminster Theological Journal* 37 (1975): 137-38.
5. So Robert W. A. Letham, 'Saving Faith and Assurance in Reformed Theology: Zwingli to the Synod of Dort', 2 vols, (Ph.D. dissertation, University of Aberdeen, 1979), 1:125-26.
6. Roger Nicole, 'John Calvin's View of the Extent of the Atonement', *Westminster Theological Journal* 47 (1985): 208. For a similar word of caution see Hans Boersma, 'Calvin and the Extent of the Atonement', *Evangelical Quarterly* 64:4 (1992): 334 and 334 n. 4.

the atonement merely because they want to claim him for their own theology. In reality, matters are more complicated than that. There is evidence in Calvin that both 'sides' can claim as their own, evidence of two kinds. First, there are statements concerning the extent of the atonement itself. Calvin's commentaries contain some passages that favor limited atonement, but the data is insubstantial.[7] Conversely, James W. Anderson has marshaled evidence from Calvin's sermons and has argued that he taught an unlimited atonement.[8] An important point that will be developed later, but that is worth mentioning now, is that scholars rarely appeal to the *Institutes* when arguing Calvin's position. The *Institutes* seems to offer little help in determining Calvin's view.

The second kind of evidence adduced by those who claim that Calvin advocates a view on the extent of the atonement is from systematic theology. Scholars point to doctrines taught by Calvin that seem to fit very well with limited or unlimited atonement, respectively. Those espousing unlimited atonement point to 'universal' themes in Calvin: his affirmation of the importance of evangelism and clear belief in a universal and free offer of the gospel.[9] Those committed to limited atonement cite Calvin's 'particular' themes: his assertion of double predestination and his emphasis on the efficacy of Christ's saving work.[10]

The existence of these two themes of particularism and universalism in Calvin's thought is undeniable. But the interpretation of the significance of them is hotly debated. Some have concluded that these two strains are hopelessly in conflict, so that 'the reformer left to his successors a theology that was... inherently unstable'.[11] This view is to be rejected because it fails

---

7. Calvin's commentary on 1 John 2:2. For a denial that Calvin here taught limited atonement, see Anderson, 'The Grace of God', p. 111.
8. Anderson, 'The Grace of God', pp. 112f., 117, 127, 129-32, 134f., 137 and 141.
9. See Calvin's commentaries on Matt. 20:28, Rom. 5:18, and Gal. 5:12.
10. See *Institutes* III. xxi, II. xvii. 4, and Calvin's commentaries on Isa. 53:11 and Heb. 8:4.
11. G. M. Thomas, *The Extent of the Atonement: A Dilemma for*

to do justice to Calvin as a clear and careful thinker. It fails to see the compatibility between particularism and the universal preaching of the gospel. Instead, I prefer to view the two strains in Calvin as a reflection of the Bible's own antinomy between divine sovereignty and human responsibility.[12] I also regard the appeal to these systematic themes as insufficient to decide the question of Calvin's view on limited/unlimited atonement. The very fact that scholars have to appeal to systematic theology hints at a paucity of actual statements in Calvin on the issue of the extent of the atonement and should serve to make us examine whether or not Calvin answers the questions that we ask.

Where, then, do I stand? I have resisted the temptation to read my view into Calvin. I hold to a position of limited atonement, but continue to think that the evidence is too ambiguous to allow a definitive answer to the question of what Calvin thinks on the matter. At the same time I acknowledge the universalist and particularist strains in Calvin's thought mentioned in the previous two paragraphs. I understand how scholars can claim Calvin as an advocate of either limited or unlimited atonement by emphasizing the particularist or universalist strain, respectively. Nonetheless, I think that it is a mistake to do so. I therefore belong to the third camp above: I confess uncertainty concerning Calvin's position on the extent of the atonement.

Nevertheless, my views have changed somewhat since I wrote *Calvin's Doctrine of the Atonement* in 1983.[13] Perhaps the most important recent contribution concerning Calvin's view on the extent of the atonement is Jonathan H. Rainbow's dissertation, 'Redemptor Ecclesiae, Redemptor Mundi: An Historical and Theological Study of John Calvin's Doctrine of the Extent of Redemption.'[14]

Reformed Theology from Calvin to the Consensus (1536-1675) (Carlisle, Cumbria: Paternoster, 1997), p. 34.

12. For a discussion of these themes in Scripture, especially the Gospel of John, see D. A. Carson, *Divine Sovereignty and Human Responsibility: Biblical Perspectives in Tension* (Grand Rapids: Baker, 1981, 1994).

13. Phillipsburg, New Jersey: Presbyterian and Reformed, 1983.

14. See note 2 for a full citation.

Rainbow argues that Calvin agrees with his historical antecedents Augustine, Gottshalk, and his contemporary Bucer in advocating limited atonement. According to Rainbow, Calvin taught that Christ, by making a definite atonement, was redeemer of the church. In gospel proclamation and pastoral work, however, Calvin presents Christ as redeemer of the world, meaning all kinds of people, not each and every person. Rainbow's scholarship is impressive. He shows that Calvin stands in a particularist tradition stretching from Augustine to Bucer, with whom Calvin served in Strasbourg from 1538-1541. Rainbow also argues convincingly that limited atonement harmonizes well with Calvin's doctrine of salvation.

Nevertheless, I am not persuaded that it is proper to claim Calvin as an advocate of particular redemption. Rainbow's argument can be turned against him at points. For example, if Bucer did teach limited atonement in his refutations of Anabaptist teaching, as Rainbow demonstrates, and if Calvin was influenced by this, then why does Calvin not give the doctrine a more prominent place in his teaching? Above all, why does Calvin not even mention the extent of the atonement when he summarizes his views on the person and work of the mediator in the *Institutes*? Rainbow's answers to this last question fall short of the mark.[15]

Although I reject his major thesis, that Calvin clearly taught limited atonement, Rainbow's work has changed my thinking. I can no longer maintain, as I did in 1983, that the extent of the atonement was not an issue until after Calvin. Rainbow convinces me that Gottshalk and Bucer (in debates with Anabaptists) taught limited atonement before Calvin.[16] I must modify my judgment, therefore, and argue that limited/unlimited atonement was not a debated issue within *reformed* circles until the time of Calvin's successor, Beza. I thus agree with Robert Letham that the extent of the atonement 'only became a major issue in the next generation'.[17] The debate over this matter waited until Moses

15. Rainbow, 'Redemptor Ecclesiae, Redemptor Mundi', pp. 364-71.
16. Ibid., pp. 67-84, 128-157.
17. Letham, 'Saving Faith and Assurance in Reformed Theology', 1.125.

Amyrald and John Cameron began promoting unlimited atonement and thereby precipitated responses from the defenders of reformed orthodoxy. Hence the question of Calvin's view of the extent of the atonement is somewhat anachronistic.

An important methodological consideration, too often overlooked, should be taken into account. Advocates of the three viewpoints generally agree that there is too little evidence in the *Institutes* to reach a conclusion on the extent of the atonement. The lack of evidence in the *Institutes* should make us cautious when using the commentaries and sermons to determine whether Calvin teaches limited or unlimited atonement. In his preface to the reader in the 1559 *Institutes*, Calvin gives his own methodological statement that one should interpret his commentaries doctrinally on the basis of the *Institutes*.[18] The conclusion, therefore, must be that it is uncertain what position Calvin would have taken if he were living at the time of the debates over the extent of the atonement.

One more point needs to be made. I am persuaded that it is fair to say that limited atonement fits better with the system of Calvin's thought than does unlimited atonement. Paul Helm, Roger Nicole, and above all, Jonathan Rainbow demonstrate that the features of Calvin's thought cohere very well with the position of particular atonement.[19] I would go so far as to conclude that limited atonement, as framed by Calvin's successors, is a valid theological extension of his own theology. But I still maintain that it is unwise to ask what is Calvin's view on the extent of the atonement, because it was a question that he did not address.

Having considered the matter of the extent of the atonement in Calvin, we are ready to summarize his understanding of Christ's saving work. There is much benefit to be derived from a study of

---

18. *Institutes*, 'John Calvin to the Reader' (pp. 4-5 of the McNeill edition).
19. Paul Helm, *Calvin and the Calvinists* (Edinburgh: The Banner of Truth Trust, 1982); Nicole, 'John Calvin's View of the Extent of the Atonement', pp. 220-25; Rainbow, 'Redemptor Ecclesiae, Redemptor Mundi', pp. 159-311.

Calvin's doctrine of the atonement. His starting point for soteriology is worthy of note. Calvin begins with the free love of God in Jesus Christ. God loved his people who deserved only his wrath. Calvin always ties God's love to Christ. Christ is the supreme manifestation of God's love and in his death for sinners he accomplished salvation.

Augustine and Bernard of Clairvaux are examples of previous writers who stressed the love of God in salvation. Calvin stands in their train when he emphatically begins his doctrine of reconciliation with God's love. The fact that Calvin chooses the love of God as the starting point for his doctrine of the atonement gives a certain coloring to that doctrine. He does not begin with speculation regarding God's eternal counsels. He does not start with an abstract discussion of God's being and attributes. He begins with God's love in Christ. For Calvin to begin in this manner is to write GOD'S GRACE in large letters over his entire doctrine of salvation. God's love is displayed in the redemption of sinners. The human response to such a gracious salvation can only be gratitude and love: gratitude toward God who loved his people before the foundation of the world, and love for him who did not spare his own Son, but gave him up for us all (Rom. 8:32).

Calvin's example should remind theologians today that the love of God in Christ should be prominent in any explication of the atonement. Beginning one's doctrine of salvation with God's love points the doctrine in a practical direction. It makes soteriology understandable to the common man or woman. God loved us and gave his Son to die in our place; this is the greatest incentive to Christian living.

Calvin is a pastoral theologian, who in the midst of intense Christian service in Geneva perfects the *Institutes* and writes the commentaries. It is therefore not surprising that his theology tugs at the heart, as well as challenges the mind. Would that theologians today would use their academic tools to make God's Word serviceable to Christians. Too frequently theologians write only for other theologians and this is one reason why Christian book stores are stocked with books that are long on popular appeal but short on substance. Calvin calls us to both intellectual integrity and practical application.

Calvin's stress on the love of God would enhance preaching today. People of the twenty-first century need to hear the Good News of Jesus Christ as much as those of the sixteenth century did. Preachers would do well to preach God's judgment against sin, God's redeeming love in Christ, and the forgiveness of sins available to all who believe on Christ. And they would also do well to communicate clearly and consistently that the Christian life is not a self-help program. God has not saved us by his grace and left us to struggle on our own. Instead, his Word makes perfectly clear, as Calvin saw plainly, that we are saved once and for all by grace through faith and that we are to live the Christian life in the same way. There is no other antidote to sin than the Holy Spirit's application to us of the death and resurrection of the Son of God. Christians need to be taught to forsake gimmicks and quick fixes to the problem of sanctification and instead to practice living by faith in God's Son, whose grace is greater than all our sins.

The atonement was the work of the God-man Jesus Christ. Calvin holds to the Chalcedonian view of the person of Christ. He gives a soteriological direction to the traditional Christology. The motive of the incarnation was redemption. Calvin affirms the full deity of Christ, for only God could save his people from their sins. He is equally emphatic about Christ's genuine humanity, which established a fraternity between him and us. This fraternity assured that the salvation Christ achieved was for us; it was our salvation because it was accomplished by a human being. Calvin ties together the person of Christ and his saving work.

This aspect of Calvin's work speaks to us today. The reformer demonstrates an historical awareness that we would do well to imitate. He is aware of patristic Christology. He understands the teaching of the councils of Nicea and Chalcedon. Too many modern students of theology lack historical moorings. Calvin encourages us to gain an understanding of the history of Christian doctrine.

Of course, theologians today must do more than merely recite the doctrinal formulations of the past. Indeed, they must speak the truth of God to their contemporaries. But when they neglect historical theology, they cut themselves off from the wisdom of the ages and consign themselves to theological faddishness.

Great benefits would accrue to the church if modern theologians would follow Calvin in beginning Christology from above, with the Second Person of the Trinity, who becomes incarnate. Too frequently moderns begin from below with Jesus of Nazareth. Consequently, often they are not able to rise above the earth. They present Jesus as the greatest human being with a unique relationship to God, but he can only be greater than we in degree, and not in kind. He is not the incarnate God-man, but only a divinized man. It is no wonder that many today have lost interest in matters pertaining to salvation. For such a 'Christ' is not able to save sinners.

Calvin's stress on the unity of Christ's person and work is valuable. Pastors would do well to synthesize Christian doctrine for their people. Too many Christians have a fragmentary knowledge of their faith; they lack understanding of how teachings fit together. Among other things, our churches need a revival of the teaching of systematic theology from the pulpit and in Sunday School. In the post-modern world at the turn of the century, Christians need to learn biblical truth in order to live for God. They are bombarded with moral relativism and need to learn to evaluate experience on the basis of biblical doctrine. If their pastors don't help them, who will?

One way in which Calvin teaches the unity of the Mediator's person and work is by using the concept of Christ's threefold office. Calvin does not originate the idea of the threefold office. Eusebius, Chrysostom, and Aquinas all spoke of Christ as prophet, priest, and king.[20] But Calvin's use of the *munus triplex* is unique. His work became a standard part of Reformed theology. Christ is the great prophet who proclaimed the Good News on earth and who continues to do so from heaven through his Spirit, whom he

20. John F. Jansen, *Calvin's Doctrine of the Work of Christ*, pp. 30f.

has poured out upon his ministers. He teaches both outwardly and inwardly. Jesus makes effectual within his hearers' hearts the message that he causes to fall upon their ears. Christ is the messianic king who maintains the salvation of his people by protecting them from their foes. He leads Christians in victory even in the midst of life's hardships. Christ is the great high priest who accomplished reconciliation for his people by offering himself to God on the cross. He continues his priestly ministry in heavenly intercession for his own. For Calvin, Christ's person (prophet, king, and priest) and work (proclamation, protection, and reconciliation) are inseparable.

Practical use of Christ's threefold office would enrich Christian ministry today. The concept of Christ as teacher working through his ministers can strengthen preachers. The people of God need to know that Christ is their king, who leads them to victory. The gospel can be clearly explained in sacrificial terms with Christ as priest who lays down his life for sinners. Just as Calvin joins Christ's person and work, Christian leaders would do well to train themselves and their people to always hold together who Christ is and what he has done for us.

Besides using the threefold office of Christ, Calvin also employs six biblical themes of the atonement to depict Christ's saving work.[21] He is not without theological precedent in his use of these pictures of reconciliation. Irenaeus emphasized Christ's obedience in his doctrine of recapitulation.[22] Athanasius wrote of Christ's saving work as a victory.[23] Augustine appreciated the

21. Tice errs when he concludes that these themes are the result of 'a projection of systematic theology back onto Calvin'. Rather, they are pictures that Calvin found in Scripture itself. (Jonathan Tice, 'The Structure and Evolution of Calvin's Doctrine of the Atonement', in *Church History*, ed. John Henry Morgan. Church Divinity Monograph series, Bristol: Wyndam Hall Press, 1991, p. 69).

22. Irenaeus, *Against Heresies* in *The Ante-Nicene Fathers*, eds. A. Roberts and J. Donaldson, 10 vols, (Grand Rapids: Eerdmans, 1884), 1:445-46 (3. 18. 1).

23. Athanasius, *On the Incarnation of the Word* in *Christology of the*

sacrificial aspects of the atonement.[24] And the apostolic fathers use the exemplary theme.[25] Nonetheless, Calvin combines the various themes and thereby summarizes the Christian doctrine of the atonement arguably better than anyone before him. Jesus is the obedient second Adam, the victor, the legal substitute, the sacrifice, our merit, and, lastly, an example in his death on the cross.

I have taught adult Sunday School for the past twenty years. This has enabled me to keep in touch with Christian lay people. I have learned that, in general, Christians are aware of only two biblical pictures of redemption. If you asked them how Jesus saves us from our sins, they would give two answers. First, they would say that he paid the penalty for our sins. Second, they would say that he saves us by offering himself as a sacrifice to God. These answers are correct. But these two pictures only provide a partial understanding of Christ's saving work. Christians' understanding would be enhanced were they to discover what Calvin saw in Scripture four hundred-fifty years ago: in addition to being legal substitute and sacrifice, Christ is also second Adam, our champion, our righteousness, and our example. I have no doubt that the faithful teaching of these atonement motifs would result in greater gratitude for grace received and greater impetus for Christian service.

Calvin's awareness of the patristic tradition and his deep respect for the teaching of Holy Scripture give a freshness to his doctrine of the atonement. He never formulates a theory of the work of Christ as, for example, Anselm did in *Cur Deus Homo*. Instead, Calvin is content to present Christ's work in terms of the threefold office and the biblical pictures. He is not afraid to leave rough edges in his presentation of the doctrine of the atonement. He allows the themes of reconciliation to overlap, even as they

---

Later Fathers, eds., E. R. Hardy and C. C. Richardson, LCC vol. 3 (Philadelphia: Westminster, 1954), pp. 63-64.

24. Augustine, Homilies on 1 John in *Augustine: Later Works*, ed., John Burnaby, LCC vol. 8 (Philadelphia: Westminster, 1955), p. 263.

25. See J. N. D. Kelly, *Early Christian Doctrines* (New York: Har-Row, 1960), pp. 163-66.

do in Scripture. In the *Institutes*, Calvin combines the motifs of obedience and victory:

> Accordingly, our Lord came forth as true man and took the person and the name of Adam in order to take Adam's place in obeying the Father, to present our flesh as the price of satisfaction to God's righteous judgment, and, in the same flesh, to pay the penalty that we had deserved. In short, since neither as God alone could he feel death, nor as man alone could he overcome it, he coupled human nature with divine that to atone for sin he might submit the weakness of the one to death; and that, wrestling with death by the power of the other nature, he might win victory for us.[26]

He also joins the images of Christ our merit, Christ our legal substitute, and Christ our sacrifice:

> But when we say that grace was imparted to us by the merit of Christ, we mean this: by his blood we were cleansed, and his death was an expiation for our sins.... If the effect of his shedding of blood is that our sins are not imputed to us, it follows that God's judgment was satisfied by that price.... For he sets Christ over against all the sacrifices of the law, to teach that what those figures showed was fulfilled in him alone.[27]

And he blends the Christus victor, sacrificial, and legal pictures:

> But we should especially espouse what I have just explained: our common nature with Christ is the pledge of our fellowship with the Son of God; and clothed with our flesh he vanquished sin and death together that the victory and triumph might be ours. He offered as a sacrifice the flesh he received from us, that he might wipe out our guilt by his act of expiation and appease the Father's righteous wrath.[28]

This phenomenon of allowing the themes of the atonement to overlap is evident in Calvin's commentaries and treatises too.[29]

---

26. *Institutes* II. xii. 3.
27. Ibid., II. xvii. 4. 28. Ibid., II. xii. 3.
29. Calvin's commentaries on Acts 4:12, 8:32, Rom. 3:24, and Gal. 2:21, and Calvin's treatise, 'Reply to Sadolet', in *Calvin: Theological Treatises*, ed. J. K. S. Reid (Philadelphia: Westminster, 1954), p. 235.

It is important to realize that Calvin nowhere attempts to relate the threefold office of Christ to the biblical pictures of the atonement. Rather, he is content to allow them to exist side-by-side. That is an example of Calvin's refusing to overly systematize doctrine. He does not start with a systematic conception of the Christian faith and then proceed to verify that system with scriptural references. He tries earnestly to be a biblical theologian. As a result, he sometimes leaves rough edges in his doctrinal formulations. So it is with his doctrine of the atonement. That is evident not only from his refusing to relate Christ's offices to the redemption motifs, but also from the overlapping he permits between offices and motifs and between the motifs themselves. The priestly office overlaps the sacrificial picture of the atonement. There is an overlap between the kingly office and the theme of victory. The biblical pictures of the atonement sometimes infringe upon one another. As a result, there is common material between Christ as obedient second Adam, Christ in his 'active' obedience in the legal theme, and Christ our merit.

Calvin unites Christ's threefold office and the biblical themes of Christ's work to form a sweeping presentation of the atonement. The offices and themes can be likened to the colors of light in the spectrum. When the various colors combine, they produce white light, and this light enables us to see clearly. Similarly, Calvin's kaleidoscopic combination of offices and themes helps readers to see more clearly the significance of Christ's saving work. Few figures in the history of the Christian church bring together as much data in their soteriology as does Calvin. He is, therefore, an important source for anyone desiring in short compass to obtain a grasp of the Christian doctrine of the atonement. *Institutes* II. xii-xvii constitutes an excellent primer for any student of the doctrine of Christ's work.

Calvin's use of the biblical images of reconciliation demonstrates the breadth of his doctrine of the atonement. Although he regards Christ's death on the cross as the central atoning act, Calvin, like Athanasius, Augustine, and Aquinas before him, considers many aspects of Christ's experience redemptive. The earthly life of Christ is redemptive, for he unites us with God and acquires righteousness for us with God 'by the whole course of his obedience'.[30] Acknowledging various redemptive elements in Christ's saving work does not detract from the importance of the cross for Calvin: 'Yet to define the way of salvation more exactly, Scripture ascribes this as peculiar and proper to Christ's death.'[31] Calvin comments on John 19:30, 'the whole accomplishing of our salvation and all the parts of it are contained in His death.'[32]

Christ's burial has redemptive significance for Calvin: 'There follows in the Creed: "He was dead and buried." Here again is to be seen how in every respect he took our place to pay the price of our redemption.'[33]

The resurrection of Jesus Christ also constitutes a part of his saving work:

> Next comes the resurrection from the dead. Without this what we have said so far would be incomplete. For since only weakness appears in the cross, death, and burial of Christ, faith must leap over all these things to attain its full strength.... We are said to 'have been born anew to a living hope' not through his death but 'through his resurrection' (1 Pet. 1:3). For as he, in rising again, came forth victor over death, so the victory of our faith over death lies in his resurrection alone.[34]

At times Calvin considers the redemptive significance of Christ's death and resurrection separately:

> Therefore, we divide the substance of our salvation between Christ's death and resurrection as follows: through his death, sin was wiped out and death extinguished; through his resurrection, righteousness

---

30. *Institutes* II. xvi. 5.
31. Ibid.
32. Cf. Calvin's commentary on Eph. 5:2.
33. *Institutes* II. xvi. 7.
34. Ibid. II. xvi. 13. Cf. Calvin's commentaries on Matt. 16:20 and 2 Tim. 2:8.

> was restored and life raised up, so that – thanks to his resurrection – his death manifested its power and efficacy in us.[35]

Nevertheless, according to the reformer, Christ's death and resurrection are inseparable in the plan of redemption:

> So then, let us remember that whenever mention is made of his death alone, we are to understand at the same time what belongs to his resurrection. Also, the same synecdoche applies to the word 'resurrection': whenever it is mentioned separately from death, we are to understand it as including what has to do especially with his death.[36]

Calvin also regards the ascension of Jesus Christ as having saving significance:

> From this our faith received many benefits. First, it understands that the Lord by his ascent to heaven opened the way into the heavenly kingdom.... Secondly, as faith recognizes, it is to our great benefit that Christ resides with the Father. For, having entered a sanctuary not made with hands, he appears before the Father's face as our constant advocate and intercessor.... Thirdly, faith comprehends his might, in which reposes our strength, power, wealth, and glorying against hell.[37]

The final act of salvation will be the second coming of Christ:

> Yet his kingdom lies hidden in the earth, so to speak, under the lowness of the flesh. It is right, therefore, that faith be called to ponder that visible presence of Christ which he will manifest on the

---

35. *Institutes* II. xvi. 13. Cf. Calvin's commentary on 1 Cor. 15:3f.
36. *Institutes* II. xvi. 13. Cf. Calvin's commentary on 1 Cor. 15:3f.
37. *Institutes* II. xvi. 16. Cf. Calvin's commentary on John 20:17. Timothy P. Palmer concurs, 'Because it was through our flesh that atonement was made and because this flesh is now in heaven, we have access to the Heavenly Kingdom.' 'John Calvin's View of the Kingdom of God' (Ph.D. dissertation, University of Aberdeen, 1988), 142. See also Randall C. Zachman, 'Jesus Christ as the Image of God in Calvin's Theology,' *Calvin Theological Journal* 25 (1990): 59.

> Last Day.... From thence we are commanded to await him as our Redeemer....[38]

The classic statement of the breadth of Calvin's doctrine of the atonement occurs in *Institutes* II. xvi. 19:

> We see that our whole salvation and all its parts are comprehended in Christ. We should therefore take care not to derive the least portion of it from anywhere else. If we seek salvation, we are taught by the very name of Jesus that it is 'of him' (1 Cor. 1:30). If we seek any other gifts of the Spirit, they will be found in his anointing. If we seek strength, it lies in his dominion; if purity, in his conception; if gentleness, it appears in his birth. For by his birth he was made like us in all respects (Heb. 2:17) that he might learn to feel our pain (cf. Heb. 5:2). If we seek redemption, it lies in his passion; if acquittal, in his condemnation; if remission of the curse, in his cross (Gal. 3:13); if satisfaction, in his sacrifice; if purification, in his blood; if reconciliation, in his descent into hell; if mortification of the flesh, in his tomb; if newness of life, in his resurrection; if immortality, in the same; if inheritance of the Heavenly Kingdom, in his entrance into heaven; if protection, if security, if abundant supply of all blessings, in his Kingdom; if untroubled expectation of judgment, in the power given him to judge. In short, since rich store of every kind of goods abounds in him, let us drink our fill from this fountain, and from no other.[39]

Perhaps no one has done a better job than Calvin of presenting the breadth of the work of Christ. Many Christians think only of the cross when they consider Christ's saving work. Preachers, therefore, would do well to teach their people all the redemptive elements in Christ's experience.

It is worthwhile to explore Calvin's use of the theological concept of satisfaction. Here I must retract much of what I wrote in 1983:

---

38. *Institutes* II. xvi. 17.
39. Ibid., II. xvi. 19.

> Contrary to the opinion of some, Calvin was not largely dependent upon Anselm in this.[40] Calvin's employment of satisfaction was his own. They are more correct who understand Calvin as overstepping Anselm and going back to a patristic idea of satisfaction.[41] Yet that thesis too can be overdone. It is most accurate to say that Calvin, although building upon a patristic base, developed his own doctrine of satisfaction. Calvin used *satisfactio* in an imprecise sense. This is evident from his refusal to tie it down to any one theme of the atonement. Instead, satisfaction was used to express salvation in terms of various themes.... Thus Calvin did not confine satisfaction to any one theme of the atonement. Rather he used the word in an imprecise and general sense to speak of the efficacy of Christ's work. It was Calvin's way of summing up the saving accomplishment of Christ. When he wrote that Christ accomplished satisfaction, he meant that the Lord Jesus did all that was necessary to deliver sinners from their plight.[42]

Upon further reflection, I now maintain that Calvin does build upon Anselm's idea of satisfaction, but moves beyond Anselm and develops his own view, which was to become standard in reformed Christianity.

Anselm of Canterbury (c. 1033-1109) had one of the most fertile minds of the Middle Ages. His famous work, *Cur Deus Homo*, *Why God Became a Man*, represents a great advance in the understanding of the atonement. Various strains of thought on the work of Christ were current in the early church, including ideas

---

40. Cf. Boniface A. Willems and Reinhold Weier, *Soteriologie von der Reformation bis zur Gegenwart*, p. 25, and François Wendel, *Calvin: Origins and Development of His Religious Thought*, p. 219. For Anselm's use of *satisfactio* see *Cur Deus Homo*, book 1, chapters XI and XIX.
41. Cf. Robert S. Franks, *A History of the Doctrine of the Work of Christ,* 2 vols (London: Hodder and Stoughton, 1918), 1:429.
42. *Calvin's Doctrine of the Atonement*, 1st ed. pp. 91-93. I was following the views of Professor Bard Thompson, Dean of the Graduate School of Drew University, in my discussion of Calvin's use of *satisfactio.*

of sacrifice, victory, suffering, and deification.[43] The prevalent idea in the west by Anselm's time was the *Christus Victor* motif, especially a version of it that held that Christ's death was a ransom paid to the devil. Gregory of Nyssa, for example, spoke of God's deception of the devil by using Christ's humanity as bait to lure the evil one. Satan gulps down the bait (puts Christ to death) only to find himself caught and hanging on the hook with the divine Logos playing the line.[44] The ransom to Satan theory of the atonement, held sway until Anselm's day.

This sets the stage for a description of Anselm's tremendous accomplishment. In *Why God Became a Man*, Anselm opposes the ransom to Satan view of the atonement and puts in its place the satisfaction theory. Satan has no proper claim on human beings and God does not owe Satan anything, Anselm insists, except punishment![45] The cross is not God's way of paying off the devil. Indeed, the cross is not primarily directed toward the devil, but toward God himself.

Anselm portrays the relations between God and humankind with images drawn from the feudal world he inhabits. God is the great Lord of the manor. Adam, as God's servant, owes allegiance and faithfulness to God and God alone. In the Fall the first man offends the divine honor, by not paying God his due. This offense against God puts man in a terrible plight, out of which he is not able to extricate himself. Hence, if man is ever to be delivered, God must take the initiative.[46] This is exactly what God does in the incarnation of his Son.

It is necessary for God to become a man if humanity is to be delivered. Christ must be God, because only God is able to save. Christ must also be a human being, because it is appropriate that

---

43. See H. E. W. Turner, *The Patristic Doctrine of Redemption* (London: A. R. Mobray, 1952) and J. N. D. Kelly, *Early Christian Doctrines*, pp. 163-88, 375-99.
44. Kelly, *Early Christian Doctrines*, pp. 380-82.
45. Eugene Fairweather, ed., *A Scholastic Miscellany: Anselm to Ockham* (New York: Macmillan, 1970), pp. 107-110 (I:vii).
46. Ibid., 134-46 (I: xix-xxv).

man, through whom the fall came, be the one to solve the problem. But no mere human being is qualified to do so. Hence the necessity of Christ's being God and man.[47] This is why God becomes a human being—to rescue errant humanity.

Anselm depicts the need for Christ's work in a formula that poses a dilemma: either satisfaction or punishment. Either satisfaction must be rendered to the offended divine honor or the requisite punishment must be endured.[48] The way God chooses is the former: satisfaction. This is what the God-man accomplishes: by offering his divine nature to God in death he satisfies God's honor and thereby restores what is lost in the fall. Although his human obedience is owed to God, his voluntary divine sacrifice is not and therefore constitutes a work of supererogation. God is thus able to reward the surplus of Christ's merit to all those who believe in him for salvation.[49]

Calvin follows Anselm in his basic outline when he speaks of Christ's work as a satisfaction. In the *Institutes* Calvin agrees with Anselm that satisfaction is made by the God-man.

> The priestly office belongs to Christ alone because by the sacrifice of his death he blotted out our guilt and made satisfaction for our sins (Heb. 9:22).... In Christ there was a new and different order in which the same one was to be both priest and sacrifice. This was because no other satisfaction adequate for our sins, and no man worthy to offer to God the only-begotten Son, could be found.[50]

Calvin differs from Anselm, however, in at least two important respects. First, Calvin does not regard satisfaction as due the divine honor, but the divine justice manifested in righteous wrath. Very often, therefore, Calvin uses satisfaction to convey the outcome of Christ's propitiating the Father's wrath. In *Institutes* II. xvi. 1 he explains:

---

47. Ibid., 150-55 (II: vi-ix).
48. Ibid., 118-22 (I: xi-xiii).
49. Ibid., 134-36 (I: xix), 150-55 (II: vi-ix), 172-81 (II: xvii-xix).
50. *Institutes* II. xv. 6.

> No one can descend into himself and seriously consider what he is without feeling God's wrath and hostility toward him. Accordingly, he must seek ways and means to appease God – and this demands a satisfaction. No common assurance is required, for God's wrath and curse always lie upon sinners until they are absolved of guilt.[51]

Secondly, Calvin differs from Anselm in that he rejects the dilemma, 'either satisfaction or punishment', and puts in its place the notion of satisfaction via punishment. In the *Institutes* Calvin teaches that Christ satisfies God by suffering the penalty that we owed because of our sins.

> I take it to be a commonplace that if Christ made satisfaction for our sins, if he paid the penalty owed by us, if he appeased God by his obedience – in short, if as a righteous man he suffered for unrighteous men – then he acquired salvation for us by his righteousness.[52]

Many times, therefore, satisfaction is Calvin's way of communicating Christ's saving work in legal terms. In *Institutes* II. xvi. 5 he teaches:

> To take away our condemnation, it was not enough for him to suffer any kind of death; to make satisfaction for our redemption a form of death had to be chosen in which he might free us both by transferring our condemnation to himself and by taking our guilt upon himself.[53]

Fifteen years have passed since the publication of *Calvin's Doctrine of the Atonement*. During that time I have been privileged to teach the topics of the Person and Work of Christ to seminary classes thirty times. What is my current estimation of Calvin's presentation of Christ's saving work? I am grateful for those who have advanced our state of knowledge beyond that presented by Calvin in the *Institutes*, commentaries, and sermons.

---

51. Cf. *Institutes* II. xvi. 6 and Calvin's commentary on 1 John 2:1.
52. *Institutes* II. xvii. 3.
53. Cf. *Institutes* II. xvi. 1, 2 and II. xvii. 3 and Calvin's commentary on Rom. 4:25.

Chief among twentieth century books on the atonement from which I have profited are Emil Brunner's *The Mediator*, Gustaf Aulén's *Christus Victor*, Leon Morris' *The Apostolic Preaching of the Cross*, G. C. Berkouwer's *The Work of Christ*, H. D. McDonald's *The Atonement of the Death of Christ*, John Stott's *The Cross of Christ*, and Robert Letham's *The Work of Christ*.[54]

Each of these authors adds to our understanding of Christ's atonement. And each (with the exception of Aulén, whose book suffers accordingly) benefits from and interacts with Calvin's ideas on the work of Christ. In other words, the very books that carry the discussion beyond Calvin rely on him in order to do so. It is legitimate, therefore, to label Calvin's presentation of Christ's saving work *classic*. Calvin's doctrine of the atonement is biblically sound, theologically synthetic (pulling together various strands of biblical and historical theology), and comprehensive (he combines threefold office, biblical themes, and more).

I. John Hesselink, the author of a valuable recent study – a commentary on Calvin's First Catechism – sums up matters well:

> It should be clear that Calvin's understanding of the atonement is very complex.... There is a breadth and sophistication in his treatment of this theme beyond that of Aquinas or Luther. Consequently, Robert Culpepper, who is not altogether sympathetic to Calvin's view, still concludes that 'Calvin's doctrine of the atonement is truly a milestone in Christian theology.'[55]

---

54. Emil Brunner, *The Mediator* (London: Lutterworth, 1934); Gustaf Aulén, *Christus Victor* (first published in 1931; reprint New York: Macmillan, 1969); Leon Morris, *The Apostolic Preaching of the Cross*. 3rd ed. (Grand Rapids: Eerdmans, 1965); G. C. Berkouwer, *The Work of Christ*. Studies in Dogmatics (Grand Rapids: Eerdmans, 1965); H.D. McDonald, *The Atonement of the Death of Christ* (Grand Rapids: Baker, 1985); John Stott, *The Cross of Christ* (Downers Grove, IL: InterVarsity, 1986); and Robert Letham, *The Work of Christ*. Contours of Christian Theology (Downers Grove, IL: InterVarsity, 1993).
55. I. John Hesselink, ed., *Calvin's First Catechism: A Commentary*, Columbia Series in Reformed Theology (Louisville: Westminster John Knox, 1997), pp. 124-25.

SELECTED BIBLIOGRAPHY

Bibliographies

Bainton, Roland H., and Gritsch, Eric W. *Bibliography of the Continental Reformation: Materials Available in English.* 2nd ed., rev. and enl. Hamden, Conn.: Archon Books, 1972.

Barth, Peter. 'Fünfundzwanzig Jahre Calvinforschung 1909-1934.' *Theologische Rundschau,* n.s. 6 (1934): 161-74, 246-67.

Battles, Ford Lewis. 'The Future of Calviniana.' In *Renaissance, Reformation, Resurgence: Papers and Responses Presented at the Colloquium on Calvin and Calvin Studies Held at Calvin Theological Seminary on April 22 & 23, 1976,* edited by Peter DeKlerk, pp. 133-73. Grand Rapids: Calvin Theological Seminary, 1976.

Cadier, Jean. 'Bibliographie Calvinienne 1959.' *Etudes Théologiques et Religieuses* 35 (1960): 205-17.

DeKlerk, Peter. 'Calvin Bibliography 1972.' *Calvin Theological Journal* 7 (1972): 221-50.

__________. 'Calvin Bibliography 1973.' *Calvin Theological Journal* 9 (1973): 38-73.

__________. 'Calvin Bibliography 1974.' *Calvin Theological Journal* 9 (1974): 210-40.

__________. 'Calvin Bibliography 1975.' *Calvin Theological Journal* 10 (1975): 175-207.

__________. 'Calvin Bibliography 1976.' *Calvin Theological Journal* 11 (1976): 199-243.

__________. 'Calvin Bibliography 1977.' *Calvin Theological Journal* 12 (1977): 164-87.

__________. 'Calvin Bibliography 1978.' *Calvin Theological Journal* 13 (1978: 166-94.

__________. 'Calvin Bibliography 1979.' *Calvin Theological Journal* 14 (1979): 187-212.

__________. 'Calvin Bibliography 1980.' *Calvin Theological Journal* 15 (1980): 244-60.

__________. 'Calvin Bibliography 1981.' *Calvin Theological Journal* 16 (1981): 206-21.

__________. 'Calvin Bibliography 1982.' *Calvin Theological Journal* 17 (1982): 231-47.

__________. 'Calvin Bibliography 1983.' *Calvin Theological Journal* 18 (1983): 206-224.

__________. 'Calvin Bibliography 1984.' *Calvin Theological Journal* 19 (1984): 192-212.
__________. 'Calvin Bibliography 1985.' *Calvin Theological Journal* 20 (1985): 268-280.
__________. 'Calvin Bibliography 1986.' *Calvin Theological Journal* 21 (1986): 194-222.
__________. 'Calvin Bibliography 1987.' *Calvin Theological Journal* 22 (1987): 275-294.
__________. 'Calvin Bibliography 1988.' *Calvin Theological Journal* 23 (1988): 195-221.
__________. 'Calvin Bibliography 1989.' *Calvin Theological Journal* 24 (1989): 278-299.
__________. 'Calvin Bibliography 1990.' *Calvin Theological Journal* 25 (1990): 225-248.
__________. 'Calvin Bibliography 1991.' *Calvin Theological Journal* 26 (1991): 389-411.
__________. 'Calvin Bibliography 1992.' *Calvin Theological Journal* 27 (1992): 326-352.
__________. 'Calvin Bibliography 1993.' *Calvin Theological Journal* 28 (1993): 393-419.
__________. 'Calvin Bibliography 1994.' *Calvin Theological Journal* 29 (1994): 451-485.
__________. 'Calvin Bibliography 1995.' *Calvin Theological Journal* 30 (1995): 419-447.
Fields, Paul. 'Calvin Bibliography 1996.' *Calvin Theological Journal* 31 (1996): 420-463.
__________. 'Calvin Bibliography 1997.' *Calvin Theological Journal* 32 (1997): 370-394.
Dowey, Edward A. 'Studies in Calvin and Calvinism Since 1948.' *Church History* 24 (1955): 360-67.
------------. 'Studies in Calvin and Calvinism Since 1955.' *Church History* 29 (1960): 187-204.
Erichson, Alfredus, ed. *Bibliographia Calviniana: Catalogus chronologicus operum Calvini; Catalogus Systematicus Operum quae Sunt de Calvino, cum Indice Auctorum Alphabetica.* 1900. Reprint. Nieuwkoop: B. de Graff, 1960.
Fraenkel, Peter. 'Petit supplement aux bibliographies calviniennes, 1901-1963.' *Bibliothèque d'Humanisme et Renaissance* 33 (1971): 385-414.
Kempff, Dionysius. *A Bibliography of Calviniana*, 1959-1974. Leiden: Brill, 1975.
Lang, August. 'Recent German Books on Calvin.' *Evangelical Quarterly* 6 (1934): 64-81.

McNeill, John T. 'Fifty Years of Calvin Study (1918-1968).' In *John Calvin: The Organiser of Reformed Protestantism*, 1509-1564, by Williston Walker, pp. xvii-lxxvii. New York: Schocken, 1969.
------------. 'Thirty Years of Calvin Study.' *Church History* 17 (1948): 207-40; 18 (1949): 241.
Nicole, Roger. 'Some Notes towards a Bibliography of John Calvin.' *Gordon Review* 5 (1959): 174-81; 6 (1960): 21-28.
Niesel, Wilhelm. *Calvin-Bibliographie, 1901-1959*. München: C. Kaiser, 1961.
Parker, T. H. L. 'A Bibliography and Survey of the British Study of Calvin, 1900-1940.' *Evangelical Quarterly* 18 (1946): 123-31.
Rowe, Kenneth E. *Calvin Bibliography*. Madison, N.J.: Drew University, 1967.
Rückert, Hanns. 'Calvin-Literatur seit 1945.' *Archiv für Reformationsgeschichte* 50 (1959): 64-74.
Tylenda, Joseph N. 'Calvin Bibliography, 1960-1970.' *Calvin Theological Journal* 6 (1971): 156-93.
Vogelsanger, Peter. 'Neuere Calvin-Literature.' *Reformatio* 8 (1959): 362-66.

Primary Sources

Collected Works

Ioannis Calvini Opera quae supersunt omnia. Edited by Johann Wilhelm Baum *et al.* 59 vols. in 26. Corpus Reformatorum, vols. 29-87. Brunswick: C. A. Schwetschke and Sons, 1863-1900.
Joannis Calvini Opera Selecta. Edited by Peter Barth, W. Niesel, and D. Scherner. 5 vols. München: C. Kaiser, 1926-52.

Institutes

Institutes of the Christian Religion. Edited by John T. McNeill. 2 vols. The Library of Christian Classics, vols. 20-21. Philadelphia: Westminster, 1960.
Institution de la Religion Chrestienne. Edited by Jean-Daniel Benoit. 5 vols. Paris: J. Vrin, 1957-63.
Institution of the Christian Religion, 1536. Translated and edited by F. L. Battles. Atlanta: John Knox, 1975.

Treatises

Calvin: Theological Treatises. Edited by J. K. S. Reid. The Library of Christian Classics, vol. 22. Philadelphia: Westminster, 1954.

Commentaries

Calvin's [New Testament] Commentaries. Edited by David W. Torrance and Thomas F. Torrance. 12 vols. Grand Rapids: Eerdmans, 1960-72.
Commentaries on the Book of the Prophet Daniel. Translated by Thomas Myers. 2 vols. Grand Rapids: Eerdmans, [1948].

Commentaries on the First Book of Moses, Called Genesis. Translated by John King. 2 vols. Grand Rapids: Eerdmans, [1948].

Commentaries on the Twelve Minor Prophets. Translated by John Owen. 5 vols. Grand Rapids: Eerdmans, [1950].

Commentary on the Book of Psalms. Translated by James Anderson. 5 vols. Grand Rapids: Eerdmans, 1949.

Commentary on the Book of the Prophet Isaiah. Translated by William Pringle. 4 vols. Grand Rapids: Eerdmans, [1948].

Secondary Sources

Anderson, James William. 'The Grace of God and the Non-elect in Calvin's Commentaries and Sermons.' Th.D. dissertation, New Orleans Baptist Theological Seminary, 1976.

Armstrong, Brian. 'The Concept of Restoration/Restitution in Calvin.' In *Calvinus Servus Christi.* Budapest: Wilhelm Heinrich Neuser, 1988. Pp. 143-150.

Aulén, Gustaf. *Christus Victor: An Historical Study of the Three Main Types of the Idea of the Atonement.* Translated by A. G. Hebert. New York: Macmillan, 1969.

Barth, Karl. *La Confession de foi de l'église: Explication du Symbole des Apótres d'après le catechisme de Calvin.* Neuchâtel: Delachaux et Niéstlé, 1943.

Battles, Ford Lewis. 'God was Accommodating Himself to Human Capacity.' *Interpretation* 31 (1977): 19-38.

Bell, M. Charles. 'Calvin and the Extent of the Atonement.' *The Evangelical Quarterly* 55 (1983): 115-123.

Berkouwer, G. C. *The Person of Christ.* Studies in Dogmatics. Grand Rapids: Eerdmans, 1954.

------------. *The Work of Christ.* Studies in Dogmatics. Grand Rapids: Eerdmans, 1965.

Blaser, Klauspeter. *Calvins Lehre von den drei Ämtern Christi.* Theologische Studien, vol. 105. Zürich: EVZ-Verlag, 1970.

Boersma, Hans. 'Calvin and the Extent of the Atonement.' *The Evangelical Quarterly* 64 (1992): 333-355.

Brenton III, Robert M. 'Calvin's Confession of Christ's Descent into Hell in the Context of the Doctrine of Redemption: an Historical and Hermeneutical Inquiry.' Th.M. thesis, Calvin Theological Seminary, 1993.

Carson, D. A. *Divine Sovereignty and Human Responsibility: Biblical Perspectives in Tension.* Grand Rapids: Baker, 1981, 1994.

Conditt, Marion W. 'More Acceptable than Sacrifice: Ethics and Election as Obedience to God's Will in the Theology of Calvin.' Th.D. dissertation, University of Basel, 1973.

Culpepper, Robert H. *Interpreting the Atonement.* Grand Rapids: Eerdmans, 1966.
Dakin, Arthur. *Calvinism.* London: Duckworth, 1941.
Dankbaar, Willem F. *Calvin sein Weg and sein Werk.* Neukirchen: Neukirchener Verlag, 1959.
Dominicé, Max. *L'humanité de Jésus d'après Calvin.* Paris: Je Sers, 1933.
Dowey, Edward A. *The Knowledge of God in Calvin's Theology.* New York: Columbia U. Press, 1952.
Fairweather, Eugene, ed. *A Scholastic Miscellany: Anselm to Ockham.* New York: Macmillan, 1970.
Fiddes, Paul S. *Past Event and Present Salvation. The Christian Idea of Atonement.* Louisville: Westminster John Knox, 1989.
Foley, George C. *Anselm's Theory of the Atonement.* New York: Longman's, Green, and Co., 1909.
Foxgrover, David L. 'The Humanity of Christ within Proper Limits.' In *Calviniana: Ideas and Influence of Jean Calvin.* Edited by Robert Victor Schnucker. Sixteenth Century Essays & Studies, 10. Kirksville: Sixteenth Century Journal Publishers, 1988. Pp. 93-105.
Franks, Robert S. *A History of the Doctrine of the Work of Christ.* 2 vols. London: Hodder and Stoughton, [1918].
Ganoczy, Alexandre. *Calvin: Théologian de l'église et du ministère.* Unam Sanctam, vol. 48. Paris: Les Éditions du Cerf, 1964.
Gerber, Uwe. *Christologische Entwürfe: Ein Arbeitsbuch.* Vol. 1, *Von der Reformation bis zur dialektischen Theologie.* Zürich: EVZ-Verlag, 1970.
Gerrish, Brian A. 'Atonement and "Saving Faith".' *Theology Today* 17 (1960-61): 181-91.
Gessert, Robert A. 'The Integrity of Faith: An Inquiry into the Meaning of Law in the Thought of John Calvin.' *Scottish Journal of Theology* 13 (1960): 247-61.
Godfrey, W. Robert. 'Reformed Thought on the Extent of the Atonement to 1618.' *Westminster Theological Journal* 37 (Winter 1975): 133-71.
González, Justo L. *A History of Christian Thought.* Vol. 3, *From the Protestant Reformation to the Twentieth Century.* Nashville: Abingdon, 1975.
Hall, Charles A. M. *With the Spirit's Sword: The Drama of Spiritual Warfare in the Theology of John Calvin.* Basel Studies of Theology, no. 3. Richmond: John Knox, 1970.
Hart, Trevor. 'Humankind in Christ and Christ in Humankind: Salvation as Participation in Our Substitute in the Theology of John Calvin.' *Scottish Journal of Theology* 42 (1989): 67-84.
Hauck, Wilhelm Albert. *Christusglaube und Gottesoffenbarung nach Calvin.* Gütersloh: Bertelsmann, 1939.
Helm, Paul. *Calvin and the Calvinists.* Edinburgh: The Banner of Truth Trust, 1982.

Hesselink, I. John, ed. *Calvin's First Catechism: A Commentary*. Columbia Series in Reformed Theology. Louisville: Westminster John Knox, 1997.

Hodge, Archibald A. *The Atonement.* 1867. Reprint. Grand Rapids: Eerdmans, 1953.

Hoogland, Marvin P. 'Calvin's Perspective on the Exaltation of Christ in Comparison with the Post-Reformation Doctrine of the Two States.' Th.D. dissertation, Free University of Amsterdam, 1966.

Hunt, Robert N. C. *Calvin.* London: Centenary, 1933.

Hunter, Adam M. *The Teaching of Calvin: A Modern Interpretation.* 2nd ed. London: J. Clarke, 1950.

Jansen, John F. *Calvin's Doctrine of the Work of Christ.* London: J. Clarke, 1956.

Kehm, George H. 'Calvin on Defilement and Sacrifice.' *Interpretation* 31 (1977): 39-52.

Kelly, J. N. D. *Early Christian Doctrines.* 2nd ed. New York: Har-Row, 1958.

Kendall, R. T. *Calvin and English Calvinism to 1649*. Oxford: Oxford University Press, 1979.

Kendall, R. T. *Calvin and English Calvinism to 1649*. Carlisle, Cumbria: Paternoster, 1997.

Kratz, Wolfgang. 'Christus – Gott und Mensch: Einige Fragen an Calvins Christologie.' *Evangelische Theologie* 19 (1959): 209-19.

Leahy, Frederick S. 'Calvin and the Extent of the Atonement.' *Reformed Theological Journal* 8 (November 1992): 54-64.

Leith, John H. 'Creation and Redemption; Law and Gospel in the Theology of John Calvin' in *A Reexamination of Lutheran and Reformed Traditions*, vol. 3, pp. 43-53. New York: Published jointly by representatives of the North American Area of the World Alliance of Reformed Churches Holding the Presbyterian Order and the U.S.A. National Committee of the Lutheran World Federation, 1965.

Letham, Robert W. A. 'Saving Faith and Assurance in Reformed Theology: Zwingli to the Synod of Dort.' Ph.D. dissertation, University of Aberdeen, 1979. 2 vols. 1:113-141; 2:60-97.

Lightner, Robert P. *The Death Christ Died: A Case for Unlimited Atonement.* Des Plaines, Ill: Regular Baptist Press, 1967.

Mackintosh, H. R. *The Doctrine of the Person of Jesus Christ.* International Theological Library. New York: Scribner, 1930.

McDonald, H. D. 'Models of the Atonement in Reformed Theology.' In *Major Themes in the Reformed Tradition.* Edited by Donald K. McKim. Eugene, Oregon: Wipf and Stock, 1998.

Menno Simons. *Complete Writings.* Translated by Leonard Verduin. Edited by John C. Wenger. Scottdale, Pa.: Herald Pr., [1956].

Milner, Benjamin Charles. *Calvin's Doctrine of the Church.* Studies in the History of Christian Thought, vol. 5. Leiden: Brill, 1970.

Morris, Leon. *The Cross in the New Testament.* Grand Rapids: Eerdmans, 1965.
Mülhaupt, Erwin. *Die Predigt Calvins, ihre Geschichte, ihre Form und ihre religiösen Grundgedanken.* Berlin: DeGruyter, 1931.
Murray, John. 'Calvin on the Extent of the Atonement.' *The Banner of Truth* 234 (March 1983): 20-22.
Nicole, Roger. 'John Calvin's View of the Extent of the Atonement.' *Westminster Theological Journal* 47 (1985): 197-225.
Niesel, Wilhelm. *The Theology of Calvin.* Translated by H. Knight. Philadelphia: Westminster, 1956.
Oberman, Heiko A. 'The "Extra" Dimension in the Theology of Calvin.' *The Journal of Ecclesiastical History* 21 (1970): 43-64.
Palmer, Timothy P. 'John Calvin's view of the Kingdom of God.' Ph.D. dissertation, University of Aberdeen, 1988.
Parker, T. H. L. *Calvin's Doctrine of the Knowledge of God.* Rev. ed. Grand Rapids: Eerdmans, 1959.
------------. *John Calvin: A Biography.* Philadelphia: Westminster, 1975.
------------. *The Oracles of God: An Introduction to the Preaching of John Calvin.* London: Lutterworth, 1947.
Paul, Robert S. *The Atonement and the Sacraments: The Relation of the Atonement to the Sacraments of Baptism and the Lord's Supper.* New York: Abingdon, 1960.
Rainbow, Jonathan. 'Redemptor Ecclesiae, Redemptor Mundi: An Historical and Theological Study of John Calvin's Doctrine of the Extent of Redemption.' Ph.D. dissertation, University of California, Santa Barbara, 1986.
Rakow, Mary. 'Christ's Descent into Hell: Calvin's Interpretation.' *Religion in Life* 43 (1974): 218-26.
Santmire, H. Paul. 'Justification in Calvin's 1540 Romans Commentary.' *Church History* 33 (1964): 294-313.
Schellong, Dieter. *Calvins Auslegung der synoptischen Evangelien.* Edited by Ernst Wolf. Forschungen zur Geschichte und Lehre des Protestantismus, ser. 10, vol. 38. München: C. Kaiser, 1969.
Scholl, Hans. *Calvinus Catholicus: Die Katholische Calvinforschung Im. 20. Jahrhundert.* Freiburg: Herder, 1974.
Schützeichel, Heribert. *Die Glaubenstheologie Calvins.* Beiträge zur ökumenischen Theologie, vol. 9. München: M. Hueber, 1972.
Servetus, Michael. *The Two Treatises of Servetus on the Trinity.* Translated by E. M. Wilbur. Harvard Theological Studies, no. 16. Cambridge, Mass.: Harvard U. Pr., 1932.
Stadland, Tjarko. *Rechtfertigung und Heiligung bei Calvin.* Beiträge zur Geschichte und Lehre der Reformierten Kirche, vol. 32. Neukirchen-Vluyn: Neukirchener Verlag, 1972.
Staedtke, Joachim. *Johannes Calvin: Erkenntnis und Gestaltung.*

Persönlichkeit und Geschichte, vol. 48. Göttingen: Musterschmidt-Verlag, 1969.
------------. 'Die Lehre von der Königsherrschaft Christi und den zwei Reichen bei Calvin.' *Kerygma und Dogma* 18 (1972): 202-14.
Stein, Siegfried. 'Mose und Christus bei Calvin.' *Reformierte Kirchenzeitung* 88 (1938): 195-99.
Strehle, Stephen A. 'The Extent of the Atonement within the Theological Systems of the Sixteenth and Seventeenth Centuries.' Th.D. dissertation, Dallas Theological Seminary, 1980.
Thomas, G. Michael. *The Extent of the Atonement: A Dilemma for Reformed Theology from Calvin to the Consensus* (1536-1675). Carlisle, Cumbria: Paternoster, 1997.
Tice, Jonathan. 'The Structure and Evolution of Calvin's Doctrine of the Atonement: Findings from Four Documents.' In *Church Divinity, 1990/91*. Edited by John Henry Morgan. Church Divinity Monograph Series. Bristol: Wyndham Hall Press, 1991. Pp. 69-87.
Toon, Peter. 'The Significance of the Ascension for Believers.' *Bibliotheca Sacra* 141 (1984): 16-27.
Turner, H. E. W. *The Patristic Doctrine of Redemption*. London: A. R. Mobray, 1952.
Tylenda, Joseph N. 'Calvin's Understanding of the Communication of Properties.' *The Westminster Theological Journal* 38 (1975-76): 54-65.
------------. 'Christ the Mediator: Calvin versus Stancaro.' *Calvin Theological Journal* 8 (1973): 5-16.
------------. 'The Controversy on Christ the Mediator: Calvin's Second Reply to Stancaro.' *Calvin Theological Journal* 8 (1973): 131-57.
Van Buren, Paul Matthews. *Christ in Our Place: The Substitutionary Character of Calvin's Doctrine of Reconciliation*. Grand Rapids: Eerdmans, 1957.
Wallace, Ronald S. *Calvin's Doctrine of the Christian Life*. Grand Rapids: Eerdmans, 1959.
------------. *Calvin's Doctrine of the Word and Sacrament*. Grand Rapids: Eerdmans, 1957.
Wendel, François. *Calvin: Origins and Development of His Religious Thought*. Translated by Philip Mairet. New York: Har-Row, 1963.
Willems, Boniface A., and Weier, Reinhold. *Soteriologie von der Reformation bis zur Gegenwart*. Handbuch der Dogmengeschichte, vol. 3, fasc. 2c. Freiburg: Herder, 1972.
Williams, George H. *The Radical Reformation*. Philadelphia: Westminster, 1962.
Willis, E. David. *Calvin's Catholic Christology: The Function of the So-called "Extra-Calvinisticum" in Calvin's Theology*. Studies in Medieval and Reformation Thought, vol. 2. Leiden: Brill, 1966.

------------. 'The Influence of Laelius Socinus on Calvin's Doctrines of the Merits of Christ and the Assurance of Faith.' In *Italian Reformation Studies in Honor of Laelius Socinus*, pp. 231-41. Edited by John A. Tedeschi. Firenze: Le Monnier, 1965.

Witte, J. S. 'Die Christologie Calvins.' In *Das Konzil von Chalkedon: Geschichte und Gegenwart*. Vol. 3: *Chalkedon Heute*, pp. 487-529. Edited by Alois Grillmeier and Heinrich Bacht. Würzburg: Echter-Verlag, 1951-54.

Wolf, Hans H. *Die Einheit des Bundes: Das Verhältnis von Altem und Neuem Testament bei Calvin*. 2nd ed. Neukirchen: Erziehungsverein, 1958.

Zachman, Randall C. 'Jesus Christ as the Image of God in Calvin's Theology.' *Calvin Theological Journal* 25 (1990): 45-62.

Index: Calvin's Institutes

Scripture Index

Luke, cont.

John

Acts

Romans

1 Corinthians

2 Corinthians

Galatians

Subject Index

Persons Index

Christian Focus Publications
publishes books for all ages

Our mission statement –

STAYING FAITHFUL
In dependence upon God we seek to help make His infallible Word, the Bible, relevant. Our aim is to ensure that the Lord Jesus Christ is presented as the only hope to obtain forgiveness of sin, live a useful life and look forward to heaven with Him.

REACHING OUT
Christ's last command requires us to reach out to our world with His gospel. We seek to help fulfil that by publishing books that point people towards Jesus and help them develop a Christ-like maturity. We aim to equip all levels of readers for life, work, ministry and mission.

Books in our adult range are published in three imprints.

Christian Focus contains popular works including biographies, commentaries, basic doctrine and Christian living. Our children's books are also published in this imprint.

Mentor focuses on books written at a level suitable for Bible College and seminary students, pastors, and other serious readers. The imprint includes commentaries, doctrinal studies, examination of current issues and church history.

Christian Heritage contains classic writings from the past.

Christian Focus Publications, Ltd
Geanies House, Fearn,
Ross-shire, IV20 1TW, Scotland, United Kingdom
info@christianfocus.com

Our titles are available from
www.christianfocus.com